CONNECTED CHRISTIANITY

DAVID SPRIGGS

CONNECTED CHRISTIANITY

Discovering the riches of the OLD TESTAMENT

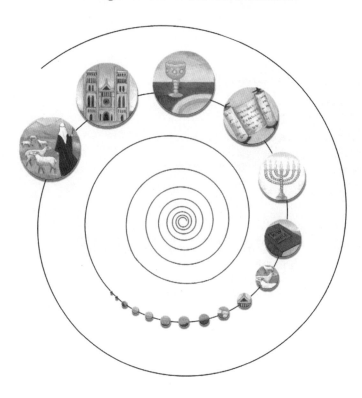

Text copyright © David Spriggs 2005
The author asserts the moral right
to be identified as the author of this work

Published by
The Bible Reading Fellowship
First Floor, Elsfield Hall
15–17 Elsfield Way, Oxford OX2 8FG
Website: www.brf.org.uk

ISBN 1 84101 420 6
First published 2005
10 9 8 7 6 5 4 3 2 1 0

Acknowledgments
Unless otherwise stated, scripture quotations are taken from the Contemporary
English Version of the Bible published by HarperCollins Publishers, copyright ©
1991, 1992, 1995 American Bible Society.

Scriptures quoted from the Good News Bible published by The Bible
Societies/HarperCollins Publishers Ltd, UK © American Bible Society 1966, 1971,
1976, 1992, used with permission.

Scripture quotations taken from The New Revised Standard Version of the Bible,
Anglicized Edition, copyright © 1989, 1995 by the Division of Christian Education
of the National Council of the Churches of Christ in the United States of America,
are used by permission. All rights reserved.

A catalogue record for this book is available from the British Library.

Printed in Singapore by Craft Print International Ltd.

CONTENTS

INTRODUCTION

Walk with me in your mind around a cathedral—you may have visited one recently. There are many fascinating features to note. We can value the different architectural styles, notice the stone and other materials from which the building has been constructed and wonder where they came from. We might reflect on the methods of construction and wonder who commissioned and funded the imposing edifice. As we wander around, the various effigies and memorials may stir our fascination with fellow human beings who lived in very different circumstances and faced different challenges. Then again, it might be the carving of the pulpit, the faded beauty of some recently rediscovered medieval wall paintings or the contemporary banners that catch our attention as we try to decipher the messages that these quite different components of the cathedral furniture seek to convey. Each of these aspects has a proper claim on our attention, and, the more background knowledge we have and the more angles we can appreciate, the deeper and richer our appreciation will be.

Now suppose that the cathedral we are visiting is one we know well. We have seen it many times and read the guide book; we have even been on the guided tour. This time, however, we are walking round it with a friend. Although we could spend many hours touring the cathedral with her, because we know she is interested in church music we concentrate on the organ, the choir stalls, the acoustics and the choral tradition of the cathedral. This is what interests our friend. Of course, the friend notices many other things too—some puzzle her, some she comments on, and we try to answer.

The Old Testament is our cathedral full of all kinds of secrets, fascinations and hidden intrigues; rich with many layers of construction; adorned with a fulsome array of art and meaning; covering many centuries of history. You may feel you know it well, that it is familiar territory and you have absorbed a great deal about it. Or you may consider yourself more like the friend being shown round, bringing your own special interests to the visit but finding the whole edifice rather overwhelming and strange.

The purpose of this approach to the Old Testament is to walk through many of its distinct parts. There will be some parts that, from our point of view, will be 'closed to the public', because the scope and nature of this book does not allow us to explore every feature of the Old Testament and associated scholarship. (So if you enjoy this study and become intrigued by it, be assured that there is much, much more to discover.) The primary purpose, though, is not to be able to say that we have seen it all, or read it all; rather, it is to increase our attentiveness—to help us see more, to learn some key questions to ask, and to provide a variety of perspectives on the Old Testament that will enrich our encounter with it when we are looking at other parts of the Bible (or, to keep to our analogy, when we visit other buildings). Then, because we have grown into a deeper appreciation of what's there and how it came to be there, we shall be able to help our friends enjoy it also, whatever their particular interests.

Before we leave our cathedral and immerse ourselves in the Old Testament, there is one more important point to draw from our analogy. As we walk round, we will sense echoes, from the past and present, that this building is the home of a community who worship God and seek to live out the life of faith, but it is possible to visit the building and miss this, its noblest feature. Until we have joined that community and experienced something of how the whole building contributes to and is enhanced by the people who worship there and the God they worship, we shall not have begun truly to appreciate that 'the cathedral' is much more than a building. So it is with the Old Testament. In the end, it is part of the foundation document of the Christian Church. In a multiplicity of ways it has nourished and challenged the faith of God's people, and through it they have glimpsed something of the glory of God. To deny this powerful aspect of the Old Testament, and forget that faith is integral to it, means that we shall miss the best it has to offer. So, we are reading it as part of Christian scripture—part of the Christian canon that nourishes the Christian community and through which we claim to discern God's revelation.

The basic Bible text used in this book is the Contemporary English Version—a recent translation based on sound scholarship, which has the approval of a wide range of churches and is noted for the clarity of its English. I hope, however, that wherever possible you will also make use of your own preferred translation. In this way your reading of the Old Testament will be enriched.

At the end of this book are questions for group discussion. They are intended to stimulate engagement with the issues raised in the book relating to the Old Testament. Even if you cannot become part of a group, you should find the questions worth pondering.

CLIFF COLLEGE

This book began life as a distance learning course on the Old Testament for Cliff College, a residential centre of training in evangelism, mission and research. Having so much enjoyed writing this course, I thought it probable that a wider audience might benefit from the work. BRF kindly agreed to publish a much-revised version and Cliff College generously agreed to allow me to reuse the materials in this way.

While Cliff College is part of the Methodist Church, it welcomes students from a wide range of denominations and backgrounds, both from Britain and Ireland and from overseas. Its courses are validated or recognized by the University of Sheffield and the college is one of seven members of the Sheffield Federation of Centres for Biblical, Theological and Mission Studies.

For further information, including details of the courses run by the college's Open Learning Centre, contact:

Cliff College
Calver
Hope Valley
Sheffield
S32 3XG

Tel: 01246 584220
www.cliffcollege.org

PART ONE

LOOKING AT THE OLD TESTAMENT

FIRST IMPRESSIONS:
THE OLD TESTAMENT AS LITERATURE

There is one very obvious difference between visiting a cathedral and looking at the Old Testament. There are many cathedrals, scattered around many countries, reflecting the many different major traditions of the Christian faith, but there is only one Old Testament. This means that when we visit, say, Exeter Cathedral, we have a general frame of reference by which to interpret it. Whether we know a lot or a little about cathedrals, their history and their architecture, this frame of reference helps us to feel at home, to recognize this particular building's strengths and strangenesses, probably without too much conscious effort. We have, however, only one Old Testament, so it is even more necessary to have some overall understanding of the plan of the Old Testament than it would be with a cathedral. The next chapter seeks to provide that overall understanding, and, by the end of that chapter, we should be able to construct a general plan of the Old Testament's parts.

First, however, we will observe some significant features of the Old Testament, both to give a sense of familiarity and to prompt us to be aware of some unusual features. We will do this by considering the Old Testament as 'literature'. This has a couple of immediate advantages. Most of us will have read books of many different kinds: novels, poetry, gardening books, biographies, car or computer manuals. We may also have studied some older literature, such as a Shakespeare play or a classic novel like Oliver Twist, in some detail. We will therefore be aware of some techniques, such as identifying metaphors, the characterization or the intrigues within the plot, which can deepen and enrich our understanding of the book. Secondly, looking at the Bible through the lens of literature is appropriate. After all, whatever else the Old Testament is, it comes to us as a written text, as literature. So what insights can we can glean from approaching the Old Testament in this way?

A familiar poem

Let us start with one of the best-known parts of the Old Testament: Psalm 23. Although the underlying image of the shepherd is less familiar to us now because most of us are not shepherds, this poem still speaks powerfully to many people. It does so because of the clarity of the images but also because many of us will have experienced this psalm in deeply moving situations such as funerals or weddings. We have also probably sung it as a hymn in various forms, and may have seen paintings that capture its moods as well.

Here it is again in a rather traditional translation (the New Revised Standard Version). Please take time to read it, allowing your imagination to be triggered by the words and to construct the images for you. Give yourself permission to make the journey of the sheep from the stream of tranquillity through the valley of dark threats and ominous dangers, and then on to restoration. Try to share something of the poet's trust in God and the restfulness that accompanies this trust. Don't rush through the psalm as something familiar, but allow yourself to pause, to digress, and to bathe in its words and form.

> *The Lord is my shepherd, I shall not want.*
> *He makes me lie down in green pastures;*
> *he leads me beside still waters;*
> *he restores my soul.*
> *He leads me in right paths*
> *for his name's sake.*
>
> *Even though I walk through the darkest valley,*
> *I fear no evil;*
> *for you are with me;*
> *your rod and your staff—*
> *they comfort me.*
>
> *You prepare a table before me*
> *in the presence of my enemies;*
> *you anoint my head with oil;*
> *my cup overflows.*

Surely goodness and mercy shall follow me
all the days of my life,
and I shall dwell in the house of the Lord
my whole life long.

As with any powerful literature, this poem can absorb us into its reality and change our moods and perspectives. It can touch deep human needs; it can extend our awareness and challenge our worldview. It engages us, delights us and moves us. This happens without our needing any detailed knowledge of shepherding or appreciation of the finer points of Hebrew poetry. The psalm works as literature.

Approaching the Old Testament along these lines produces much for ourselves, as well as to share with our friends. Indeed, several years ago, I discovered something about the 'magic' of this poem with just such an approach—something that I had not found in the many commentaries that I had read. Having once having seen it, it was obvious—but then these things usually are.

Look at Psalm 23 again. Now notice a detail, if you haven't already done so. In the first three verses, God is referred to in the third person singular, as 'he'. This gives these verses a somewhat objective and distanced view of God, even though the claims made about him are valuable and intimate. Then, in verse 4, as the storm clouds gather, there is a change to the second person singular, 'you' ('thou' in the older translations). Now, instead of God being described at a distance, he has become our companion; instead of listening to the poet's account about God, we are seeing God through the heart and eyes of the poet, listening in on his conversation with God. The grammar (the change from third to second person) mirrors the message perfectly: 'you are with me'. We experience the truth through the grammar as well as the words and images. From a literary point of view, this is one of the techniques that has made the poem so powerful.

Story

The Old Testament can also provide us with some powerful narrative material. From the many passages we could have selected, we will look at two examples. First, read Genesis 39, at least verses 6b–20. Here is a very powerful seduction scene, which could provide the script for an episode in many of our TV soaps. Neglected middle-class wife falls for her husband's protégé. When he refuses her persistent advances, she finally loses it and frames him on a rape charge, and he finds himself in prison with a very bleak future. What is worthy of note, however, is the vividness and yet simplicity with which the story is told: 'Joseph was well-built and handsome, and Potiphar's wife soon noticed him. She asked him to make love to her' (vv. 6b–7).

The scene is set clearly and quickly. Wonderful use is made of dramatic tension: 'She kept begging Joseph day after day, but he refused to do what she wanted or even to go near her' (v. 10). We are left to imagine the wife's growing desire turning to desperation, as Joseph's attempt to keep away from her—to avoid being tempted or being the cause of temptation —fuels her passion.

'One day, Joseph went to Potiphar's house to do his work, and none of the other servants were there' (v. 11). Joseph is caught—caught between the need to fulfil his responsibilities to his master and the danger of an obsessed woman. The absence of the other servants leaves him vulnerable—or perhaps provides him with the perfect opportunity to please his mistress and satisfy his own youthful passions!

Every word of this story counts, and it reads like a self-contained episode. For those who know the bigger context, it is even richer, however. Joseph's natural charisma, which makes him both his father's and his master's favourite, also brings him to this moral dilemma, for he is now his mistress's favourite. Overarching this story of charm and success, which leads Joseph to a rollercoaster ride of highs and lows, he is also God's favourite. In the end, this will prove decisive.

During his time in prison, Joseph again wins favour, this time with the guards. Through his interpretation of the baker's and wine steward's dreams, his hopes rise that he will be freed—but no, he is left in prison as the wine steward forgets Joseph after his own release. Then, the wine steward remembers Joseph's proven gift for unravelling dreams, when Pharaoh is troubled by his nightmares. Success brings Joseph to a powerful position as second-in-command of Egypt. This is not primarily for his own aggrandisement, however; it puts him in a position where he can save 'Israel'—in the form of his brothers and father (see Genesis 39—45).

As we leave the story, there are three things to remember.

- Joseph can 'save' Israel only because his righteousness leads him through great suffering—suffering that is undeserved.
- In saving Israel, he is also used by God to save Egypt: God does not save one without the other.
- In the process of saving Israel, he has to exercise costly forgiveness towards his brothers, who betrayed him into slavery.

Little wonder, then, that many Christians have seen in this story a prefigurement or reflection of the story of Jesus.

For us, the main point to note just now is that this is gracefully crafted literature, which we can appreciate and respond to without any detailed understanding of Egyptian or ancient Near Eastern history or customs. The story speaks in a universal language of passion, power and unjust suffering. Nevertheless, like any powerful and enduring literature, it also contains many layers of meaning, so that the more we know, as well as the longer we reflect on or imagine ourselves in this story, the more our appreciation grows. For instance, when Jacob gives Joseph a 'fine coat' (Genesis 37:3: whether this meant a coat of many colours or one with long sleeves is debated), his brothers understood the gift as a clear indication that Jacob intended to make Joseph his heir. No wonder they were intent on getting rid of him.[1]

To balance the books, so to speak, the story of Ruth, which depicts a woman in a much better light, paints for us a superb portrait of faithfulness, love and loyalty. It is also full of the same literary qualities as the story of Joseph—simplicity, universality, archetypal characters, courage in the face of serious adversity, a sense of journey and adventure, and love that is rewarded in the end with a dependable and generous husband. On the way, we experience many twists, turns and tensions as the story unfolds.

Fable

A third kind of literature that we may recognize in the Bible is the fable. A fable is a story, usually with animals or birds as the characters, which is used to convey a serious challenge, often by showing up the folly of human behaviour. The storyteller might use this device to say something for which otherwise he would lose his head! Here is an illustration from

Judges 9:7b–15, where we hear a story told by Jotham. He is the only son of Gideon (one of the foremost judges in Israel) who survives the mass killings instigated by Abimelech, who wants to become the king of Shechem. The context is that Jotham is challenging, even mocking, the leaders of Shechem who have decided to appoint Abimelech as their king.

Leaders of Shechem, listen to me, and perhaps God will listen to you.

Once the trees searched for someone to be king; they asked the olive tree, 'Will you be our king?' But the olive tree replied, 'My oil brings honour to people and gods. I won't stop making oil, just so my branches can wave above the other trees.'

Then they asked the fig tree, 'Will you be our king?' But the fig tree replied, 'I won't stop growing my delicious fruit, just so my branches can wave above the other trees.'

Next they asked the grape vine, 'Will you be our king?' But the grape vine replied, 'My wine brings cheer to people and gods. I won't stop making wine, just so my branches can wave above the other trees.'

Finally, they went to the thorn bush and asked, 'Will you be our king?' The thorn bush replied, 'If you really want me to be your king, then come into my shade and I will protect you. But if you're deceiving me, I'll start a fire that will spread out and destroy the cedars of Lebanon.'

The striking irony of the trees (imagine mighty oaks and cedars of Lebanon reaching upwards majestically to the sky) asking the thorn bush to be their king is hard to better. The thorn bush, meanwhile, has the audacity to say to them, 'Come into my shade.' Of course, a thorn bush doesn't provide shade for anything, least of all a real tree. And secondly, if you accepted its invitation all you would get is a face full of thorns. Imagine being embraced by that kind of bush! There is still worse to come, though, for the thorn bush can be a serious danger to the oak and the cedar: if it catches fire, as it is likely to do in a drought, it would burn so fiercely that it could ignite the whole forest.

A DEEPER CHALLENGE

Not all the literature of the Bible is so easy to appreciate. There are parts of the Old Testament which, even when we might think we recognize the type or 'genre' (the more technical term, often used by scholars), are far more difficult for us to grasp. Indeed, our lack of background knowledge can sometimes mislead us into thinking that we have made sense of it when we have missed the main points.

Poetry

Let's return to the Psalms for our first example. Take Psalm 24—the very next one after Psalm 23. It is, of course, a vibrant and challenging psalm, but in reading it some background knowledge may be helpful.

Firstly, one of the keys to Hebrew poetry is that the lines are usually in pairs, and the second line means much the same as the first, although it uses different words. So, in verse 1 of Psalm 24 we have:

> *The earth and everything on it belong to the Lord.*
> *The world and its people belong to him.*

The second line is not evidence that Israelites believed there were two worlds. Where the first line says 'everything', we are probably meant, as in the second line, to understand it to mean 'everybody', because the two lines help to shape each other's meanings.

In all probability, few people would imagine that the psalmist thought there were two planets ('earth' and 'world') but on other occasions when this same device is being used, interpreters can easily forget. For instance, many a sermon has been preached on the difference between wisdom and knowledge, or understanding and wisdom, using verses like Job 28:20 and 28 (GNB):

> *Where then is the source of wisdom?*
> *Where can we learn to understand?* …
> *To be wise, you must have reverence for the Lord.*
> *To understand, you must turn from evil.*[2]

The second of these verses actually helps us to understand that at least one component in 'reverence for the Lord' is turning from evil; whether that 'evil' should be understood in relation to issues like worshipping idols or in a moral sense can be debated.

More critical for understanding Psalm 24, however, is the recognition that it is part of a liturgical text for a procession towards the temple in Jerusalem. Some of the lines are spoken by those moving towards the city and some lines by those within it, perhaps the priests (there is, in other words, an 'antiphonal' structure to the poem), but the different speakers are not marked out for us. It is like a script in which the characters' names have been dropped from the text—and is just as difficult to read.

The psalm also becomes much more vivid and real if we remember that those approaching the city were carrying the ark of the covenant, which was closely associated with God as the 'glorious king', the one who rode at the head of Israel's army. Further background may include the idea of the surrender of a city to a conquering army. Among the messages of this psalm is the fact that, even though people are approaching the city ceremonially, carrying the powerful symbol of God's presence—with God as the conquering general, so to speak—nevertheless access will be granted only to those who are morally and spiritually right.

Texts like this show us that while we need to bring all our own literary skills and sensibilities to any text in the Bible, sometimes more background knowledge, both about the way Hebrew literature works and its historical contexts, can enrich or even correct our readings.

Genealogies

If you go round some cathedrals, you will find heraldic insignia of important families. Occasionally in churches, but more often in stately homes, you can find family trees portrayed through these heraldic devices. Heraldry is a pictorial but very precise and formal language, which tells the expert much about the status and history of any family member. There are strict rules about what devices different families are permitted to use.

Genealogies are similar in that they portray family histories, and there are many types to be found in the Bible. Probably the most famous are the two genealogies of Jesus in Matthew 2 and Luke 2. To most of us, they may seem boring and redundant. Within many societies, however, including the ones represented by the Bible, they would be fascinating and significant. We can understand something of their vital importance when we reflect that they could serve as your passport (ensuring that you were recognized as belonging to the 'right' nation or tribe). They could be your work permit (especially if you were a priest or a Levite), and they could guarantee your inheritance and land rights.

We can see some of these functions at work in a couple of biblical examples. First, let's look at Genesis 10:21–32 and 11:10—12:1. To begin with, we observe the claim that Shem was 'the ancestor of all the Hebrews' (10:21, GNB). This is picked up in 11:10, which gives more detail and, most importantly, links Shem with Abraham (11:26), who is indeed the father of Israel. Within the understanding of genealogies, this is a most important message, telling us not only that Israel is to be God's chosen people, but also that she has a real historical place among all the nations.

Secondly, we can note 10:20–31, which tell us that the different clans had lands allotted to them. If you wanted a stake in the land, you needed to be able to establish your genealogy.

Finally we can look at 10:32: 'All these peoples are the descendants of Noah, nation by nation, according to their different lines of descent' (GNB). This implies that all peoples live under the covenant established between God and Noah (Genesis 9). On one hand, the complexity of these nations establishes that God's blessing and command to have many children *all over the earth* has been fulfilled (Genesis 2:28). This is important in view of God's promise to Abraham and the delay in fulfilling it (Genesis 12:1–3). On the other hand, it means that all peoples are related and that God has their good within his view.

The second example of the significance of a genealogy comes at the end of the book of Ruth (see 4:17–22), where it instantly changes the story from being simply about tragedy and love among country folk to being the prologue to the accession of Israel's greatest king—David. This short genealogy then finds its way into Jesus' genealogy (see Matthew 1:2–6a; Luke 3:32) and, for Christians, gains even greater weight. It is an amazing 'tailpiece', indicating the foreign element in the line of Israel's most revered monarch. In the light of what at times amounts to an obsession with ethnic purity, this brief genealogy is potential dynamite, not something to be skipped over as an incidental decoration, and certainly not to be regarded as a mere literary device. Without appreciating the significance of genealogies within the Old Testament, we might well dismiss them in this way.

It is not easy for the non-expert to 'read' biblical genealogies properly. Through misunderstanding some of the basic rules, Archbishop Usher thought that he could date the origin of the earth by adding together the length of life of each generation.[3] Unfortunately, research shows (primarily by comparing different accounts of parallel genealogies) that there was no requirement to list all the generations: 'son of' can mean a distant descendant, and several generations can be missed out. The fundamental issue was not to provide the details of each generation but to establish the line of descent.

As we have already seen, genealogies in the Bible were normally about legitimizing and affirming a variety of claims. They were an important means for maintaining social stability, a way of communicating proper order and ensuring public recognition.

Once this understanding is appreciated, it makes the significance of the genealogies in Genesis spring to life, illuminating their amazing theological content. They indicate a recognition that the other nations are part of the overall 'family of God' and have their own legitimacy and territorial rights.

If we approach the genealogies superficially, reading them through our eyes, we can easily downgrade them as well as misinterpret them, because they are an alien genre for most of us.

CONCLUSION

Approaching the Old Testament as literature can be an illuminating process. It does not necessarily require specialized knowledge of the Old Testament itself, or any of the many scholarly disciplines, which in different ways can also enhance our reading. Some aspects of its literature are strange to us, however, so more background knowledge can deepen our understanding.

Having illustrated the value of reading the Old Testament in this way, we must now zoom out. We have been looking at the micro level; we need to move to the macro level, to grasp the overall plan of the Old Testament. This too will enhance our understanding.

NOTES

1 This insight also sheds a different light on the parable of the prodigal son (Luke 15:11–32). Did the elder brother think that his father was making the prodigal the inheritor when he put on him the best clothes, after all he had received and wasted, and all the disgrace he had brought on his father and the whole family?

2 Passages like Proverbs 1:2–5 and 2:9–10 show that there was a large number of terms available within Israel to denote the same range of meaning. It would be fascinating to explore why we have ended up by referring to it all as 'wisdom', with 'knowledge' and perhaps 'understanding' as equal seconds, but to do so would take us too far from the main purpose of this book.

3 Archbishop Usher (1581–1656) was an Irish cleric from Dublin, who became Archbishop of Armagh in 1625. In 1640 he settled in England, where he was favoured by Cromwell, in spite of his loyalty to the monarchy. It was in his *Annals of the Old and New Testament*, published 1650–1654, that his chronology appeared, dating creation at 4004BC.

Chapter 2

GAINING PERSPECTIVE

We began by approaching the Old Testament from the point of view of literature. This is an appropriate way to start, because the Old Testament is a written text like most literature, but it is not the same as most books we will have encountered. In this chapter we will seek some clarity about what kind of book it is.

Open your Bible and find the contents page. The list of all the books of the Old Testament alerts us immediately to a difference between the Bible and a Shakespeare play or a Dickens novel, for we are not dealing with a single book but with a small library of 39 books.

If you were a librarian with 39 books, how might you arrange them? The books of the Bible could be arranged in any of the following ways.

- **Alphabetically:** in fact, some Bible contents pages do provide an additional alphabetical listing.
- **Historically:** according to the dates they were written or the periods of history they cover.
- **By author:** listing their names either alphabetically or chronologically, according to their date of birth.
- **By genre:** fiction (fables, poetry) and non-fiction (history, biography, autobiography and so on).

Each arrangement could be helpful for different reasons. We cannot say that any particular way is 'best' until we know the purpose of the arrangement.

In what way are the 39 books of the Old Testament ordered? With such a small number, it should be easy. Let's start with how they are *not* arranged.

- They are not alphabetically ordered, neither according to the English alphabet nor in the order of the Hebrew alphabet (the language in which most of the Old Testament was written).

- They are not arranged by author. Some of the books look as though they might be, because they have people's names for titles. This does not mean, however, that the person named is the author of the book. The book of Ezra appears to be written, at least in part, by a man of that name, but Esther is a leading character in the book named after her, while the book of Joshua tells the story of Joshua and contains speeches he gave, but doesn't claim to be written by him. Many of the other books named after a person, such as Jeremiah, have content dealing with that character rather than written by them.
- They are not arranged historically, although some of the books do follow some kind of chronological order. Genesis starts with the creation of the universe (we can't get much earlier than that) and Exodus seems to pick up the story where Genesis left off, but then Leviticus, Numbers and Deuteronomy don't flow from Exodus in a straightforward way.

To make things more complicated, some of the books are actually compilations. The most obvious example is the Psalms, which contains five books, each one being a collection of very different kinds of psalms. Some of the books that we have as two in our Bibles are one in the original Hebrew, such as 1 and 2 Samuel.

While there is no easily discernible way by which the books of the Bible were arranged, this does not mean that there is no sense to the structure of the Old Testament. We cannot be sure, but we do in fact have a pretty good idea that the purpose of the arrangement was to nurture the faith of God's people. So what order do we have?

- The first five books are normally known as the Torah—the 'Books of the Law' or, to give its more technical title, the 'Pentateuch'.
- The historical books, many of which are known in Hebrew as the 'Former Prophets'.
- The Psalms.
- Wisdom material—Job, Proverbs, Ecclesiastes (together these are known as the 'Writings').
- One love song: Song of Songs (or Song of Solomon).
- The Prophets (in Hebrew they are known as the 'Latter Prophets'), including Lamentations.

Please notice that even following this order brings its problems. Ruth might well be considered as Wisdom material rather than a historical book, as indeed might Jonah, who is presented as a prophet. (Notice, by the way, that Jonah is a story about the prophet rather than a collection of the prophet's messages, or oracles, in contrast to the other prophetic books that are titled with a prophet's name, such as Hosea and Ezekiel.)

The Psalms, which are more like worship songs, interrupt the collection of Wisdom material, coming after Job and before Proverbs. Lamentations comes after Jeremiah and is followed by Ezekiel, but is clearly not a prophetic book of the same kind that they are, Some people think that Daniel is a different kind of material, called 'apocalyptic'. This is concerned with revealing matters that are otherwise hidden, including dream interpretation, but also foretelling future events.

By now, you may be thinking that the Bible is not quite such a simple book as you assumed when you started. Don't panic! It is the same when you start to look more closely at anything. Take astronomy, for instance. The night sky never looks quite the same once you become aware of the differences between the planets and the stars, or realize that the Milky Way is the edge of our own galaxy, or discover that astronomers think there is more matter in the universe that we can't see than what is visible. Increasing knowledge, awareness of complexity—or even our own confusion—should not prevent us from appreciating its overall beauty. Think back to our central analogy of the cathedral. Beginning to recognize different styles of architecture from different historical periods, or getting to know some of the varied (and not necessarily edifying) reasons for building it, should not spoil our appreciation of its wonders.

Before we continue our tour of the Bible, we should note two further features. The Roman Catholic Church includes in the Bible another group of books known as the deutero-canonical books. The canon of the Old Testament is the 39 books that we have been considering; *deutero* means 'second' or 'secondary'. Like the first set, these writings are very mixed and do not fit neatly into categories. They are Tobit, Judith, Additions to Esther, Wisdom of Solomon, Ecclesiasticus, Baruch, 1 & 2 Esdras, Letter of Jeremiah, Prayer of Azariah and Song of the three Jews, Bel and the Dragon, 1, 2, 3 and 4 Maccabees, and Prayer of Manasseh. If you have a Bible that contains these books, do sample them. Some are very important for giving us insights into the way people were thinking between the end of the Old Testament and the beginning of the New

Testament, including the way they perceived the Old Testament, and also perspectives on their history.

The other feature we need to note is that the Hebrew Bible is somewhat different in its order (as well as its categorization) from our standard English one, outlined above. The main difference is that the 'Writings' (the Wisdom books) come at the end, so that the order is Torah, Former and Latter Prophets, the Writings. Many of us will recall that in the New Testament the phrase 'the Law and the Prophets' occurs, for instance in Luke 16:16 when Jesus says, 'Until the time of John the Baptist, people had to obey the Law of Moses and the Books of the Prophets' (see also Matthew 5:17; Acts13:15). References to 'the Writings' are rare, however (see Luke 24:44). It is also the case that quotations from or allusions to these books are much less frequent, and for some scholars and interpreters this prompts the question of whether, and to what extent, these 'Writings' were regarded as authoritative in the time of Jesus.

Chapter 3

WAYS OF READING

FAMILIAR WAYS OF READING

Unless this is the first time that we have read the Old Testament, it is inevitable that we bring some presuppositions with us; we will look at it through the lenses we have acquired through all our previous encounters with it, such as Sunday school lessons, critical asides made at school, sermons, books we have read and television programmes we have watched.

For most Christians, there are three main ways in which we are likely to have been introduced to the Old Testament.

Many of us will have been told (and then read for ourselves) some of the multitude of fascinating Old Testament stories when we were children, either at Sunday school or by parents or grandparents. Such a way of absorbing the Old Testament probably means that we remember the stories out of context and value them for rather different qualities than were originally intended.

This approach has also had a profound impact on the way many preachers use the story elements within the Old Testament: focusing on the 'personalities' of the Old Testament is a common derivative, and has natural appeal for people with pastoral orientations.

Secondly, we may have been soaked in parts of the Old Testament through the liturgical traditions of the churches in which we have grown up. This can provide us with a rich reservoir of recollection, but the material will almost always have been completely cut off from its biblical context and from any historical reconstruction that might give it a connection to the real world. We do not know very much about the details of Isaiah's ministry, so sometimes scholars and preachers re-construct, or make intelligent guesses at, the background to particular sayings. Although these guesses may be inaccurate, they do at least convey the sense that Isaiah's words were spoken to specific people at a specific time: the words related to real situations. Those who absorb the

Bible, and particularly the Old Testament, by hearing parts of it read from a lectionary each week tend to see it as having an ethereal meaning, perhaps with a wonderful atmosphere of mystery, enhanced sometimes by the distancing promoted by older translations. They may even come to hold the mistaken view that the passage is best appreciated when it is functioning like music rather than communicating content.

Thirdly, we may frequently come across the Old Testament through our devotional Bible reading, through the notes we may use on a daily basis. Often these notes will provide some kind of introduction. Given the restrictions on space, however, and the need for the notes to move towards an opportunity for personal devotional response, they can lead to a privatized reading of the Old Testament, when the passage might actually be dealing with issues of very public truth, such as how to treat your military enemies or how to organize the economic system.

To find out to what extent these three ways of reading the Old Testament has affected us, we could try the following test.

- How many Old Testament stories can you recall in ten minutes?
- How many sermons can you remember hearing in the last twelve months about Old Testament personalities?
- How much Old Testament material can you recall from frequent use in church liturgy?
- If you use Bible reading notes, look back at the Old Testament sections, especially the final reflections and prayers. To what extent have they personalized public truths or events?

Of course, there are significant gains in having learnt to approach the Old Testament in any or all of these ways, not least that most of them will predispose us to valuing, as well as knowing, at least parts of the Old Testament. This very familiarity brings some dangers, however, for such approaches can lead us to focus on very limited amounts and types of Old Testament material, as well as luring us into a false sense of security about having understood the texts. Perhaps an equally insidious danger is that we read the Old Testament through recollection of its stories and characters rather than returning to and focusing on the text in all its richness. If we *think* we know what is there, we might find it hard to note what is really there. That is one advantage in using different translations or even paraphrases of the Bible: they sometimes make us 'light up' as we think, 'So that's what it was really trying to say', or even, 'What? Where did that understanding come from?'

SCHOLARLY WAYS OF READING

One of the great attributes of the historical critical approach to the Old Testament, which dominated Old Testament scholarship in the later part of the 19th and the 20th centuries, was that it trained people to look extremely closely at the text and so be alert to the possible significance of tiny details. This process developed in parallel to the analytical methodology in science, which was focusing on ever smaller details of organic as well as inorganic materials in order to understand how things worked.

One of the classic emphases of this approach was the attempt to identify different strands or strata in the books of the Bible, by noting apparent inconsistencies, repetitions and the preference for different vocabulary when describing the same reality. An obvious case was the different names used for 'God', as in the following example.

The people trembled with fear when they heard the thunder and the trumpet and saw the lightning and the smoke coming from the mountain. They stood a long way off and said to Moses, 'If you speak to us, we will listen. But don't let God speak to us, or we will die!'

'Don't be afraid!' Moses replied. 'God has come only to test you, so that by obeying him you won't sin.' But when Moses went near the thick cloud where God was, the people stayed a long way off.

The Lord told Moses to say to the people of Israel:

With your own eyes you saw me speak to you from heaven.

EXODUS 20:18–22

Notice how 'God' becomes 'the Lord' in verse 22; this is more interesting when we compare verses 18–19 with Deuteronomy 5:23–27, where the same episode is described, involving the use of both 'God' and 'the Lord'.

Starting from the different names used for God, scholars attempted to extend the range of distinguishing features (vocabulary, style, ethics, background, theology) for different strands. They distinguished the 'Yahwist' writer (who uses 'The Lord' or *Yahweh* for God's name, even before Exodus 3, where God reveals that special name to Moses) from the

'Elohist' (*Elohim* being the more general Hebrew word used for God), from the 'Deuteronomist' (whose work is mainly seen in Deuteronomy), and from the 'Priestly' source (to be found interwoven with the Yahwist and the Elohist, in the early books of the Old Testament). By using more and more criteria, scholars went on to distinguish not only different strata but different revisions of strata. Many then reached the conclusion that analysing the text in this way had several fundamental weaknesses.

First, there is the difficulty in establishing consensus as to what any source might or might not contain. How could scholars determine which sources might be put together to give a meaningful text, out of all the possible 'sub-texts'? To clarify this, let us suppose we only had four criteria: A, B, C and D. Perhaps all four could belong together; perhaps any three of them could actually combine, leaving another strata using just the remaining one; or perhaps they formed pairs, or just one pair and two single ones. Then there are other questions, such as which is older than the others, and what significance age has for authority, and so on.

More recent scholars have argued that it is possible that these 'source-critical' analysts selected their particular combinations because those combinations related (perhaps only subconsciously) to their own general philosophical presuppositions, or how they thought Israel's religion (or religions in general) had developed.

Secondly, there is the issue of whether defining sources in this way gives us a coherent story or piece of material. If not, we are left guessing at what was left out of one source when it was joined to another. Everything becomes both messy and speculative.

Thirdly, there is the presupposition that because material contains differences, or even apparent conflicts, it must come from different sources. The 'purist' scholars who have worked to discern those different sources assume that a writer has to use the same word for the same reality (whether for God, a mountain or some everyday object), or that the writer will only give one side of an argument without becoming inconsistent. But what if this kind of approach does not actually reflect the way Israelites would have done things? What if those who wrote down the texts in Israel liked combining different versions, rather as if one person combined different newspapers accounts of an event or person to give as fully rounded a picture as possible, or even because they wanted to represent the viewpoints of the different newspapers rather than what actually happened? What if this 'combining' mentality was the norm in

Israel and the 'purist' mentality wasn't? Given this scenario, would it be possible to get back to the original, separate 'newspaper' versions? The answer is 'maybe'!

The source analysts' position began to weaken further when scholars started to consider the possibility that the material in the Torah was significantly developed through Israel's worship in her sanctuaries and in connection with her festivals, before it was ever written down. The scholars who moved in this direction recognized that variations and apparent inconsistencies could then be explained in ways other than by analysing literary sources.[1]

Finally, we should consider whether the analytical approach to sources, and the scholarly reconstruction of the development of Israel's beliefs that followed, took enough account of the impact of oral tradition, in contrast to a society such as ours where writing is the norm and where we value reliability and clear official statements. Perhaps, for instance, the rules are the same as for classical poetry, which originally functioned in a largely oral society: didn't these poets strive for variety in words even when referring to the same object, because that variety gave greater pleasure to the listener?

Over recent decades, as people have attempted to understand the structural clues that suggest what features were important in Israelite discourse, including storytelling and poetry as well as traditional sayings, they have often found that what source analysis considered as different sources appears from the viewpoint of rhetorical or narrative structure to form a whole; that apparently disparate views reflect structures expressing tension and resolution, which are appropriate to narrative discourse. The various assessments of Israel's desire to have a king like the other nations provide an example of this (see 1 Samuel 8—10 and compare Deuteronomy 17:14–20).

This is not to dismiss the work of those who attempted to analyse sources using the criteria of difference. They taught us to pay meticulous attention to details; they provided us with ways of reading biblical texts which prompted us to look for the sociological or cultic[2] context out of which different voices could be heard; they may even have identified different levels of development within these texts.

When it comes to understanding an Old Testament book within the context of the whole Bible, however, we must also ask whether what really matters is the message of the whole book rather than individual strands or sources. After all, it was because of the message of the whole book that it was included in the Bible, not because of the analysed strands. It is rather like identifying some oblique reference in a T.S. Eliot poem, or the echo of a folk tune in a classical composition. Doesn't understanding the piece depend on how that reference functions in its new setting? Surely we don't need to wonder too much about the original? Put like this, the question may seem easy to answer, but it is not necessarily so simple or straightforward. For instance, perhaps T.S. Eliot wanted us to be aware of the original source in order to make sense of what he was saying. He does, after all, sometimes give us his references!

This perspective throws out a further challenge to the analysts. If an Old Testament book as a whole was meaningful both to the people who constructed it and to those who allowed it into the canon of scripture as it now stands, they must have thought that in some way it made sense—unless, of course, we are prepared to say they were all idiots, blind to details (even though they copied out manuscripts by hand with meticulous care), and that we are the only ones who can make sense of the text. If the book made sense to those who included it in the Bible, isn't our first job, as people in the community of faith with them, to try to understand what message they were getting from it? In a way, there is a parallel here with analytical scientists who, for instance, seek to understand how an animal works by dissecting its dead body. Opponents argue that this is rather pointless; should we not observe how an animal functions as a living being, in the context of its environment?

Holistic approaches become more significant when we move to studying human beings, who have potentials for self-reflection and imagination as well as for survival. They are even more critical when we come to higher-level human activities such as art, music and religion. If the Bible really is God interacting with humans and not only a human activity, it may be that God has chosen to communicate with us through this particular set of words and stories as we now have them, rather than through any dissection we choose to make—just as a composer communicates his meaning through the particular blend of themes and their developments rather than simply through individual musical notes.

As I have already suggested, it has proved illuminating for scholars to explore more deeply the connection between some parts of the Old Testament materials and Israel's ceremonies, festivals and places of worship, and we can take the psalms as a case in point. This approach is very different from the way the psalms may be used in our liturgies or services, however. For instance, in many Christian traditions they are a regular and central part of the liturgy, with perhaps two or more psalms being read or sung in a service. Although this reminds us that some of the psalms would have been used corporately and with musical accompaniment, it is not normal practice in our churches to distinguish between personal and corporate psalms, and then only to use the corporate psalms as part of the liturgy. Nor are particular psalms necessarily linked to special events in our liturgical calendar, although some may be. Instead, what often happens is that the psalms are read consecutively throughout the year, with the readings taking place at the same point each time in the liturgy. The net result can easily be that the psalms are completely dissociated from their Old Testament contexts. How many people who use the psalms in worship in this way are aware that Psalms 95 and 97—100 may have originated in a new year festival in the Jerusalem temple? Or how often, when we read Psalm 24, do we think of the ark of the covenant being involved in a procession returning to the gates of Jerusalem? Such awareness does not invalidate contemporary liturgical use; rather, it reminds us that these words could have functioned in a much richer and more varied way. Developing this awareness can even suggest more creative ways to use the psalms today.

With other Old Testament materials—such as historical or prophetic texts—that find their way into present-day liturgical use, the loss of awareness of how they functioned in their original context may be more serious. At the very least, there are insights to gain and deeper perceptions to reach by checking out the context and discovering how the texts were used by the people of Israel. It is helpful to ask ourselves what we lose and gain by the way we use such texts, compared with their original Old Testament use, and whether studying their original use can prompt us to more creative and challenging engagement with it now.

As previously mentioned, many of us have encountered the Old Testament through its 'personalities'. From Abraham to Amos, from Deborah to David, from Moses to Micah, it has been customary to engage with the Old Testament through its leading characters. Perhaps this tradition was fostered by epic biblical paintings, perhaps it owes much to the Victorians' fascination with the impact of powerful individuals, but it has certainly been a prominent dimension of Sunday school materials and church sermons. Even scholarship has not been averse to this approach.[3]

There are benefits to this kind of engagement: it tends to be memorable, and can bridge the gulf of history as we find ourselves linked by a common humanity. We should be aware, however, that a lot of the Old Testament is not primarily about 'personalities', and that God is the chief character. Many of the stories to which we might relate through the main personalities may actually be intended to teach us other lessons. Sometimes, the text does not seem intent on giving us a picture of a person so much as narrating the story or providing us with the oracles that a prophet delivered. It is often the story, or the 'words from God', that are central, and it is through the narration rather than through the personality that the message comes.

NOTES

1 For instance, some scholars think that the Sinai event as it appears in Exodus contains many hints that it was developed in the context of Israel's worship. See, for example, the German scholar Beyerlin, *Origins and History of the Oldest Sinaitic Traditions* (Blackwell, 1965).

2 'Cultic' does not mean relating to the cults, but the *cultus*: the festivals, ceremonies, sacrifices and places of worship.

3 Fleming James, *Personalities of the Old Testament* (SCM Press, 1939).

PART TWO

BEHIND THE TEXT

Chapter 4

THE OLD TESTAMENT AS A SOURCE FOR ANCIENT NEAR EASTERN HISTORY

HISTORICAL RECONSTRUCTIONS

Assyria was a powerful nation about 500 miles to the north-east of Israel's northern boundary. This nation was particularly powerful from 880 to 650BC. Sennacherib ruled Assyria as king from 705 to 681BC. There was considerable excitement when an inscription dating from his reign was found, stating:

As for Hezekiah of Judah who had not submitted to my yoke, I surrounded and captured 46 of his strong towns, the forts and uncountable smaller places in their neighbourhoods… He himself I shut up in Jerusalem, his royal city, like a bird in a cage.[1]

This inscription corroborated a long biblical narrative about Sennacherib's invasion of Judea and the siege of Jerusalem, found in 2 Kings 18—20:

In the fourteenth year of Hezekiah's rule in Judah, King Sennacherib of Assyria invaded the country and captured every walled city, except Jerusalem. Hezekiah sent this message to Sennacherib, who was in the town of Lachish: 'I know I am guilty of rebellion. But I will pay you whatever you want, if you stop your attack.'
2 KINGS 18:13–14

Such a passage is fascinating to historians of the ancient Near East for a multitude of reasons. For one thing, it means that a whole lot of archaeology can come into play. Where were there walled cities in Judah, and is there evidence (such as broken walls or burnt buildings) that they were attacked around this time? Are there any Assyrian remains buried at the correct levels? Then, the fact that Hezekiah sends messengers to Lachish suggests that there was a fairly sophisticated form of espionage going on (how did Hezekiah know where Sennacherib was?) as well as developed methods of diplomacy. Hezekiah talks about 'rebellion', so what does this imply about the way a superpower like Assyria managed their empire? When did Judah become a vassal state of Assyria, and what led them to rebel at this particular point? (See 2 Kings 18:3–8 for some hints.)

Why did Sennacherib make his headquarters at Lachish instead of pressing on to Jerusalem? What steps might Hezekiah have taken to protect Jerusalem? A clue is given right at the end of this section of Kings: 'Everything else Hezekiah did while he was king, including how he made the upper pool and tunnel to bring water into Jerusalem, is written in *The History of the Kings of Judah*' (2 Kings 20:20).

Historians know well that ensuring a water supply is absolutely essential if your city is going to withstand a siege. Fortunately, we have a very clear idea of what is being referred to in 2 Kings 20:20. The tunnel still exists, and I have walked the 550 metres or more from the Gihon spring to the Pool of Siloam. The tunnel was rediscovered in 1880 and, amazingly, an inscription was found right at the middle of the tunnel, carved in the rock. It tells how two groups of men, working from opposite ends, met up. Indeed, the slight misalignment of the two approach tunnels can still be seen. The inscription was removed 'for preservation'. Even such an inscription does not satisfy archaeologists—it could have been a fake, or a misguided inscription put in later—very recent research on the lime used to line the tunnel has established that the original dating of the tunnel is likely to be correct.

If we now look at the corresponding passages in Chronicles we can note some other features too. First, we turn to 2 Chronicles 32:32. Much in Chronicles is a copy of the same material in Kings, and at first glance, this verse appears to be a copy of 2 Kings 20:20. The reference to the tunnel is missing, however. It is tempting to think that it doesn't feature so highly in the priorities of the writer of Chronicles. These books have a somewhat different purpose from Kings, and such different perspectives always interest historians. Understanding why something was written can help us to evaluate the historical worth of a text and can also indicate how to read it to gain reliable historical information. If this was all we had from Chronicles, it might even raise in our minds the possibility that Chronicles was correcting Kings. If we didn't have the archaeological and physical evidence of the tunnel, we might wonder whether it had ever been there.

Fortunately, in this case we do have more from Chronicles. 2 Chronicles 32:30 does refer to the construction of the tunnel, and in more detail, although it doesn't give away precise information as to where it ends up in Jerusalem. Was this in case the document fell into enemy (perhaps Babylonian) hands, or because the details had been forgotten?

If we look at 2 Chronicles 32:2–4 (which has no parallel passage in 2 Kings), we learn that Hezekiah's response to the threat from Assyria was to block off all the water supplies around Jerusalem. This may relate to the tunnel, although it is not directly mentioned here. Indeed, the tunnel is mentioned not in connection with these defensive measures but later, in the context of Hezekiah's building prowess and wealth (see 2 Chronicles 32:27–29).

2 Chronicles 32:5–8 details more defensive measures that Hezekiah arranged for Jerusalem, as well as a snippet of a speech he gave to rally his troops. Then Chronicles returns to following the text of 2 Kings. What is the historian to make of all this? Is it real historical knowledge? Were details of Hezekiah's response to the Assyrian threat in *The History of the Kings of Judah*, and the author of 2 Kings chose to omit them? Or are they part of the story that the 'Chronicler' wants to tell?

Some of the points to remember from this brief incursion into the Bible as ancient Near Eastern history are as follows:

• The Bible often provides us with distinctive and detailed material that we would not otherwise know about.
• When historians are studying Old Testament texts, they do not 'privilege' them: in other words, they treat the texts as they would any other historical source, seeking to evaluate the reliability or otherwise of the material there by comparing all possible materials, including other texts and archaeology. Indeed, there is some evidence that historians are harder on the Bible than on other sources.
• The reference to *The History of the Kings of Judah* should remind us that we never have the whole picture to work with. Probably, most written records have been destroyed or lost through history. This applies to records from other nations as well as Israel. Just because there is nothing from Assyria or Babylon to confirm the interactions with Israel recorded by the Bible, it does not mean that those interactions did not happen.
• Where we can compare texts (even, as in this case, when they are both in the Bible), it is never easy to be sure what to make of the records.

Are they contradictory, supplementary or even fantasy? Inevitably there will be a 'reconstruction' in the minds of the historians, by which they reach their decisions about reliability and about which attitude to take to the text. If you have ever watched the experts on archaeological programmes such as *Time Team*, you will have seen different and often conflicting theories at work, and how they influence the way the 'hard, factual' evidence of archaeology is received.

The historical reading of the Old Testament has contributed a great deal to our ability to understand and appreciate it. When we consider texts like the Assyrian one about Sennacherib at the start of this chapter, they place the Old Testament firmly within a bigger political, historical and even geographical framework. Such understandings change and enrich our ability to appreciate the grandeur and significance of the Bible. They underline the fact that this book is about a people who had a real historical existence and who interacted with the major political and military powers of their day. The Old Testament was forged in the real world, not in a monastery or as a mystery.

We have looked at a very specific point in the history of Israel to show that what the Bible recounts does connect with verifiable historical events, but also to indicate some of the issues that emerge, even with a well-documented and archaeologically corroborated event. We have 'zoomed in', and it is now time to 'zoom out' to provide a backcloth against which to locate other material from the Old Testament, and to provide a general perspective.

HISTORY AND GEOGRAPHY

It is useful to recognize that Israel's history was strongly influenced by geography and the superpowers to the north and the south. We have already met Assyria, but before Assyria there were other powers dominating the north, such as the Hittites, and after the Assyrians came the Babylonians and the Persians. We could make a comparison with Europe over the centuries, where first one country dominates (say, France), then another (say, Germany), and then another (say, Britain). They fight among themselves as well, of course, but from time to time one or other of these nations becomes strong enough to expand and to seek for more wealth and power.

To the south of Israel was Egypt. This country too went through different phases both in terms of internal stability and territorial size, and with a succession of dynasties. Sometimes Egypt became stronger and wanted to expand to the north, although a lot of the time the attempts to push the boundary of her control northwards were intended to protect herself from the northern powers.

Where does Israel fit into this picture? Israel's territory was the corridor through which trade and armies had to pass on their way north and south. In effect, she provided the battleground where the superpowers could fight for supremacy over each other. Israel's territory also expanded and contracted, but even at its greatest it was relatively small, lying between the Mediterranean Sea on the west and the Jordan rift valley (and the associated mountain ranges) on the east. Occasionally (such as during the time of David and Solomon), Israel became a more significant local force. This was partly because the superpowers were dormant, partly because Israel's local neighbours such as Syria (to the north) and Edom (to the east) were also relatively weak, and partly because Israel herself had become stronger through military leadership, political wisdom and trade. Many Bibles include maps that can be very helpful in clarifying the relationship between Israel and the superpowers.

TIMELINE

We can also gain a sense of Israel's historical development by considering a timeline, although it is important to be aware that dating, especially in the earlier periods, is a hazardous enterprise. All dates are, of course, BC.

1900–1700	Israel's pre-history: the patriarchs
1700–1250	Israel's gestation: the time in Egypt
1250–1200	Israel's childhood: wanderings and settling in Canaan
1200–1050	Israel's adolescence: the time of the Judges
1050–950	Israel's adulthood: the period of the united monarchy
950–600	Israel's middle-age: the divided monarchy
	• 722: the northern tribes are captured by Assyria
600–500	Israel's old age: exile and return, dispersion, and Roman occupation
	• 587: the southern tribes are captured by Babylon

Israel's pre-history

For this period, we are heavily dependent on the stories about the patriarchs (Abraham, Isaac, Jacob and Joseph—together with his brothers) that we find in Genesis 12—50. These tell of large family or tribal migrations, which begin in Ur and end in Egypt with Jacob following Joseph there, around the 18th and 17th centuries BC. As an indication of the mobility of these people, it is worth pointing out that Abraham also went to Egypt (see Genesis 12:10–20).

Fixing exact chronology here is difficult, but what these stories do is to tell us not only of the beginnings of the nation but also of the faith that was to shape the whole nation and provide the material that we call the Old Testament, as well as somehow maintaining this diverse people through a complex history. Not only are Abraham, Isaac and Jacob depicted as key figures in these chapters, but they also feature in various places throughout the Old Testament and indeed the New Testament.

Scholars have done their best to reconstruct the kind of religion that the patriarchs and their people practised. One important feature is the special relationship between God and the people indicated for us in the phrase 'the God of Abraham, Isaac and Jacob' (for example, Exodus 3:16). Another characteristic is the importance of the promise of this God about the future growth of the tribe, for which the fullest illustration is in Genesis 12:1–3.

Israel's gestation

During the next 400 years or so, this small group of people developed into a much larger group, living in Egypt. Whether they could all trace their DNA back to Jacob, we have no means of telling. It is likely that other groups associated themselves with them and that marriages took place with people who were living nearby. The nomads were beginning to settle, but according to the biblical text they remained a very distinct group from the Egyptians and became a significant component of the population. Eventually they were perceived by the ruling powers as a threat, and steps were taken to subjugate them by slavery and male 'birth control' (Exodus 1:8–22).

Although we cannot be certain of the dates of Moses' birth and the exodus, they are usually located in the 13th century BC, because of the dates of the building projects. Egyptian records also tell us of other people's expulsion and migrations from that country. Strange as it may seem, though, given the amount of detail about location in the books of Exodus to Deuteronomy, we cannot be sure of the route that the Israelites took out of Egypt.

Israel's childhood

The biblical accounts tell us of a lengthy, 40-year period of wandering in the lands between Egypt and Canaan. They also tell us that this period was formative and foundational for the Israelites' whole future. The Old Testament recounts how the people were formed into a covenant community—that is, a people who had a special relationship with their God, YHWH (normally pronounced 'Yahweh': 'Jehovah' is an anglicized corruption of the word, as in Hebrew there were no written vowels). This relationship was initiated by God's gracious act of redemption of the people from Egypt, and called for worship and obedience in response. Hosea, several centuries after the exodus, puts it like this: 'The Lord says, "When Israel was a child, I loved him and called him out of Egypt as my son... Yet I was the one who taught Israel to walk"' (Hosea 11:1, 3, GNB).

Rebellion against God—expressed by breaking the covenant—was considered a particularly heinous crime and activated curses and punishments. 'If you refuse to obey my laws and commands and break the covenant I have made with you, I will punish you. I will bring disaster on you' (Leviticus 26:15–16, GNB).

This understanding of the relationship between people and God may well have been strongly influenced by a form of political arrangement that was prevalent at the time, called 'treaty', in which a powerful ruler would either impose on or offer protection to a smaller state in return for loyalty and other requirements. In the Bible, the covenant is a kind of treaty, and as part of the arrangement there were rules to govern everyday behaviour as well as worship.

Israel's adolescence

Early in the twelfth century BC, a group of tribes linked by this covenant arrangement migrated into Canaan, mainly from the south and east, and began to settle the lands on the east near the river Jordan as well as moving northwards and towards the coast. They did not take over the land completely but infiltrated it, sharing it with the inhabitants, which led to varying degrees of antagonism and violence. Israel's own version of this process is to be found in the books of Joshua and Judges. The archaeological evidence also supports this as a time of tribal migrations and transitions with a degree of violence.

By the middle of the eleventh century, Israel's next major social development took place, when Saul was anointed as king. Some of the Judges had brought together a number of tribes and led them for a time, but Saul was recognized as being a king such as the other nations had (see 1 Samuel 8:5). The advisability of moving towards monarchic rule was a serious question for the Israelite tribes. Some felt that having their own king was not only politically dangerous, as it meant centralizing power, but was also a rejection of God as their covenant king, and thus constituted rebellion. Others in Israel felt that it was necessary to have a king, to deal with the menace of the Philistines.

The Philistines were a seafaring people who had settled on the Mediterranean coast of Israel and, much like the Vikings in British history, were pushing inland, sometimes in raids and sometimes over longer periods with a slower kind of invasion. They were also more sophisticated culturally than the Israelite tribesmen, as their buildings, weaponry and pottery show, so it is tragic that the name 'Philistine' has become synonymous with a lack of artistic appreciation. Their name has also been given to the land: 'Palestine' is a variant of 'Philistine'.

Israel's adulthood

The first king to have a lasting impact on Israel and to start a dynasty (unlike the Judges and Saul) was David. The details of his story are in 1 Samuel 16—1 Kings 2. He is depicted as sorting out the Philistine menace (although early in his career he may have colluded with them, and throughout his reign he had troops and leaders of very mixed origins). Perhaps his two long-term achievements to capture Jerusalem, establishing it as his governmental and religious centre, and to solidify the relationship between the Israelite tribes.

David was followed by Solomon, whose reign saw the greatest prosperity in trade and the greatest extent of the Israelite 'empire'. His more profligate lifestyle led to antagonism between the southern tribes and the majority in the north, however, leading to the break-up of the kingdom into two parts, known as Judah (the south, including Jerusalem) and Israel (the northern and eastern tribes, whose capital became Samaria).

Israel's middle age

Relationships between the northern and southern kingdoms varied over time, depending on, among other things, the degree of pressure from the superpowers. Judah was always more likely to be responsive to pressures from Egypt in the south, and Israel to the northern superpower, whether this was Assyria or some other nation. The situation was also affected by how well the two kings of Israel got on together, which was itself often dependent on the mutuality of their power bases: if one became stronger, it might turn on the other and so weaken their mutual ability to cope with external threats.

Another factor was the influence of Jerusalem, as the religious centre, over the whole country. Sometimes Judah and Israel joined together to try to fend off a common enemy, sometimes they attacked each other and sometimes they threw in their lot with opposing superpowers. Despite all this political disturbance and disunity, however, the commitment to Yahweh united at least parts of the dispersed populations. Even here, though, there were differing and strongly held views about the degree of compatibility of Israel's religion with that of the original inhabitants of the land and with the practices of the temple in Jerusalem. Although the temple had been built there by Solomon, and was intended as a magnetic attraction for all, some questioned its legitimacy.

By 721BC, much of this became rather theoretical, because the Assyrians managed to capture most of the north and deported many of the leaders while importing other peoples from different parts of their empire. This practice was their usual approach to controlling conquered peoples, and it meant the end of the ten northern tribes as a religious and political component of the original Israel. Not surprisingly, those left in the north who had Israelite connections contested this separation, but more and more of these people became viewed with suspicion by those in the south, and eventually became known, by the time of Jesus, as the

Samaritans. They had further developed their own sacred places, and some even came to view themselves as the true Israel.

From 721 to 597BC, Judah strove to keep her independence by forming all manner of political and military alliances, but in the end she was no match for the superpowers and was attacked by the Babylonians. Jerusalem was sacked and the leaders of the population deported to Babylon. Strangely, this did not mean the end of Judah, as the Assyrian attack had largely meant for the ten northern tribes.[2] Rather, this became a time when the people started to collect their scriptures and found alternative ways to preserve their faith and nationhood. Indeed, within a relatively short period, some of the leadership was able to return from Babylon and initiate the rebuilding of Jerusalem, the temple and the community. Some of these developments can be followed in the books of Ezra and Nehemiah, while prophets like Haggai and Zechariah also contribute to the picture.

These developments were possible because Babylon had been dethroned as the world power by the Persians. By now, though, 'Israel' was no longer confined to her former territory, but her peoples were present in wider Asia as well. At the same time there was a tendency for these peoples to become more exclusive and to reject the allegiance proffered by the peoples left in the northern part of the country.

Israel's old age

These experiences of being subject to foreign intervention and dispersion, and the attempt to preserve the people as a religious community, continued over the next four centuries. The Persians were followed by the Greeks and then the Romans as the dominant superpower. As always, there were struggles nearer home as well, with sometimes the Egyptians and sometimes the Syrians having a significant effect on Israel's life. In the middle of the second century BC, and for around 100 years afterwards, there was a period of Jewish independence, but that was very much a relative term.

Throughout these centuries, there was a growing sense that Jews dispersed throughout the empires, along with a tendency for those in and around Jerusalem to consider themselves the élite, the real people of God. Some people tended to assimilate with the cultures around them, while others strove for religious purity and hence separation as far as possible from alien influences, and still others longed for (and often fought for) political independence. To a considerable extent, our views of these years depend on whose story we listen to. Most of the deutero-canonical books were written during this period, but it was also during this time that the majority of the Old Testament reached its present form. The fact that the text was preserved throughout these tumultuous times is itself an amazing fact, bearing witness to the energetic faith of the community.

Eventually, around AD70, Rome lost patience with the Jews in Israel and Jerusalem was besieged and sacked yet again. The temple was brutally destroyed and has never been rebuilt. But this historical event means that we have leap-frogged those few years which, although they were politically and militarily insignificant, Christians regard as the pivot of all history, namely the birth, ministry, death, resurrection and ascension of Jesus.

This, then, in outline, is a reconstruction of nearly two millennia of history as it relates to the people who are both the key human subjects of and the originators of the Old Testament texts as we have them. No reconstruction can tell the whole story, but such an account is offered, like a cathedral guidebook, to help you keep your bearings as you look more closely at specific parts of the building. It can also help you if you want to find the shortest route to another part.

NOTES

1   Quoted from *The Lion Handbook to the Bible* (3rd edn, 1999), p. 301.
2   By this period, 'Israel' in the Old Testament can mean the two remaining tribes of Judah. Taking this name was a way of claiming all the historical traditions and religious significance of the twelve tribes for the southern kingdom—rather like Jacob stealing Esau's birthright (see Genesis 27).

Chapter 5

THE RELIGIOUS LIFE: SACRIFICES AND FESTIVALS

For many people, trying to understand the set-up of a cathedral can be difficult. We might well recognize the pulpit and even the lectern, but the altars, the choir stalls and the seats reserved for various dignitaries might confuse us, as well as the side chapels devoted to Mary or other saints. There may be parts of the building that, because we don't have clues to their spiritual significance from our own experiences, we gloss over or simply appreciate on aesthetic grounds.

When we approach the Old Testament, many of us are likely to be in this kind of situation. The feasts, festivals, sanctuaries and sacrificial systems were a fundamental part of Israel's worship and communal life, but to us they are so alien that we can easily miss their true significance. To some of us, they might even be rather offensive, perhaps because of the animal slaughter involved. Our understanding is not always helped by the New Testament's verdict on the sacrificial system (see the letter to the Hebrews, for instance) as having been dispensed with by the death of Christ. Some of us may have an ingrained antagonism to anything that mentions sacrifice, as being too 'catholic'. If we have any of these perspectives, it is understandable that we may struggle to appreciate how central and valuable Israel's 'cultic' worship was to her communal identity. (Remember that the word 'cultic' relates to Israel's places and activities of worship, festivals and sacrifices.)

Nevertheless, anyone who wants to understand the Old Testament at all must stop, look, listen, feel and explore these areas of its life. Even if we struggle to view certain texts sympathetically, we still need to give them full attention and withhold our natural tendency to reject things that we do not easily understand or value. In doing so, we will not only 'get inside' the Old Testament, but we will also come to appreciate the New Testament and our faith more fully.

OBJECTIONS TO SACRIFICES?

First, however, we need to take a brief look at some Old Testament passages that, confusingly, seem to condemn sacrifices. We find one of the most striking of these in Hosea 6:6: 'For I desire steadfast love and not sacrifice, the knowledge of God rather than burnt offerings' (NRSV).[1]

Amos 5:22, 25 is even more forthright: 'I won't accept your offerings or animal sacrifices—not even your very best... Israel, for forty years you wandered in the desert, without bringing offerings or sacrifices to me.' Jeremiah closely follows Amos, both in God's rejection of sacrifices and in claiming that Israel was not asked to offer sacrifices during the wilderness wanderings: 'I won't accept sacrifices from you. So don't even bother bringing them to me... At the time I brought your ancestors out of Egypt, I didn't command them to offer sacrifices to me' (Jeremiah 7:21–22).

Even one of the psalms makes a similar statement, but this time from the viewpoint of the worshipper. 'Offerings and sacrifices are not what you want. The way to please you is to feel sorrow deep in our hearts. This is the kind of sacrifice you won't refuse' (Psalm 51:16–17). The fact that this comes in a psalm that includes several cultic references (such as 'wash me with hyssop', v. 7) may give us reason to pause before leaping to the conclusion that the surface meaning of the texts above is the correct one—namely, that God neither values nor asks for sacrifices at all.

On the surface we apparently have God completely rejecting sacrifices as a requirement in Hosea, Amos and Jeremiah's time, coupled with the claim that in the wilderness (the early days, when God's revelation was clearest or Israel's relationship with God at its purest) sacrifice was not required.

How can we understand these texts in the light of the significant emphasis on sacrifice that appears elsewhere? To give one example from many throughout Exodus to Deuteronomy, in Exodus 20:24 we read, 'Build an altar out of earth, and offer on it your sacrifices of sheep, goats, and cattle.'

It could be that the prophets were mistaken in thinking that God had not requested or commanded sacrifices while Israel was on her way from Egypt to Canaan. This would imply, however, that they did not know the first five books of the Bible in anything like the form we have them today.

It could be that they were using history in a polemical way—implying through their reading of history that sacrifice was not fundamental to life with God, because what mattered was obedience to the communal and social aspects of God's requirements. Amos uses Israel's sense of privilege in a similarly polemical way when he says that just as God rescued or 'brought up' Israel from Egypt, he also 'brought up' the Philistines (Israel's arch-enemies) from Crete (Amos 9:7).

Perhaps it was particular kinds of sacrifice—associated with Canaanite practices—that were being rejected, rather than all sacrifices. Certainly, in Hosea and Amos the prophets frequently complain that Israel's worship is so confused with Baalism that it is useless. In the time of Jeremiah, people were offering their sacrifices to pagan divinities and in pagan ways. Accordingly, the reference to the wilderness in Jeremiah 7 might be in connection with Israel's sacrifices to the golden bull that they had made (see Exodus 32): God did not command such sacrifices.

It could be that the emphasis of the prophetic texts is on the phrase 'bringing them to me': understood this way, they might imply the rejection of a corrupt priesthood not fit to offer sacrifices (compare 1 Samuel 2:12–17). According to Jeremiah 7:16–19, not even the intercessory prayer of the prophet would have any beneficial effect: the people had put themselves beyond the boundaries of the covenant and only within such boundaries did sacrifice or prayer have validity.

Maybe Hosea 6:6 really means that it is not sacrifice as such that God rejects, but sacrifice without the right attitudes of repentance and covenant love, as Psalm 51 suggests and Micah 6:6–8 also states. Or perhaps the sacrifices were not valid because the place where the sacrifices were offered was no longer pure or even available. That is one way to read Psalm 51:18–19: 'Please be willing, Lord, to help the city of Zion and to rebuild its walls. Then you will be pleased with the proper sacrifices, and we will offer bulls on your altar once again.'

THE IMPORTANCE OF SACRIFICES AND FESTIVALS

However we handle these points (and there is, in my opinion, no easy solution),[2] we must also recognize that the sacrifices and the festivals of which they were a part were of considerable significance to Israel, if we reflect on texts in the Torah and the historical books as well as the Psalms.

Indeed, the importance of the sacrificial system and the festivals can be reckoned from the amount of text given over to them, and from the intricacy of the details provided. For example, take a quick look at Leviticus 16—17 and 22—24. There are also comprehensive passages about the construction and furnishings of the tent of meeting, including the ark of the covenant, and about the behaviour of the priests in all kinds of contexts, including what clothes they are to wear (see Exodus 25—40 and elsewhere).

It is also worth noting that the requirements about sacrifice and festivals are interspersed with passages about personal and community behaviour: Leviticus 19 starts with a couple of the Ten Commandments, moves on to details about sacrifices, then defends the disabled, demands impartial justice, and commands that 'foreigners' are to be loved as much as Israelites love themselves. All of this suggests not only that sacrifices and festivals were important but also that they were very much integrated within the whole Israelite way of life. There is little evidence of a sacred–secular divide here, or that the religious aspects of life were considered a harsh imposition on ordinary people by a domineering and oppressive priesthood.

A further indication of the significance of sacrifices and festivals is seen in the fact that they are presented as part of the overall covenant deal, although slightly removed from the revelation at Sinai. Leviticus 1:1 states, 'The Lord spoke to Moses from the sacred tent and gave him instructions for the community of Israel to follow when they offered sacrifices.' Chapter 40 of Exodus concludes with God's glory being revealed within the sacred tent, and is best understood as a recapitulation of the first revelation at Sinai. Perhaps this distinction reflects the tradition that God did not ask sacrifices from Israel 'in the wilderness' (Amos 5:25; Jeremiah 7:22) but only wanted them to take place once Israel was in the land.

Yet another indication of the significance of festivals and sacrifices is the way that they are often integrated with Israel's historical traditions. (By 'historical traditions', scholars mean the frequent and various ways in which the Old Testament relates stories or narratives to explain Israel's existence, her relationship with God and her situation in Canaan.) This integration is probably seen best in Deuteronomy 26:1–11, but it occurs elsewhere, such as Exodus 12. In Deuteronomy 26, when the worshipper presents the harvest offering, he is required to recite a summary of the history of Israel, from Abraham, through to the oppression in and deliverance from Egypt and the arrival in the promised land. Israel's historical journey as a nation and their sacrificial life are closely united.

On reflection, the heavy significance of sacrifices, festivals, priests and places and equipment for worship should not surprise us. After all, the first of the Ten Commandments tells people to worship God alone and not to worship idols, and all of these details relating to the cult are really focused on ensuring that Israel does just that.

FESTIVALS

Within the scope of this book, we are going to restrict our attention to the annual festivals. One reason for selecting them is that whereas many of the general instructions in Leviticus are directed to 'Aaron and his sons, the priests' (Leviticus 21:1, 16–17; 22:1–2, 17–18), the instructions for the festivals are addressed 'to the community of Israel' (see, for example, 23:1–2, 9–10, 33–34). Even with this rather restricted subject, we will limit ourselves to two approaches. Firstly, we will look briefly at several festivals, to give us a sense of their overall scope. In this way we can see how they gave structure to the annual life of an agricultural people, as well as providing some kind of cohesion for the different tribes. Secondly, we will look in more detail at one of the festivals, the Festival of Shelters, and follow some of its development through the Old Testament.

The most succinct statement about festivals is found in Deuteronomy 16. Verse 16 reads, 'Each year there are three festivals when all Israelite men must go to the place where the Lord chooses to be worshipped. These are the Festival of Thin Bread, the Harvest Festival, and the Festival of Shelters.'

It is easy to relate this verse to the preceding verses in connection with the Harvest Festival and Festival of Shelters, which are named in verses 9–15, but 'Thin Bread' comes as something of a surprise. With a closer reading of verses 1–8 we can identify Thin Bread with the Passover, but this prompts the question, why call the festival 'Thin Bread' when it is actually the Passover?

It is interesting to compare these verses with similar passages in Exodus, where there are two references to the three annual festivals. The closest passage is 23:14–17, with a briefer version in 34:23. If the context for the latter is examined, references to Thin Bread, Harvest and Shelters can be found, but the arrangements are very different from those in the Deuteronomy passage. The references occur after a variety of injunctions aimed at keeping Israel's worship distinct from her neighbours', linked to a version of the first of the Ten Commandments. There are also references to redeeming the firstborn and limiting work to six days, though no reference to sabbath observance itself. The reference to Passover (Exodus 34:25), as distinct from Thin Bread, is almost a passing one—the tail-piece to an instruction not to use bread made with yeast when sacrificing an animal.

All of these pointers and others have suggested to scholars that the Festival of Thin Bread was at one time separate from Passover. Such observations are reinforced when scholars view them through the lens of comparative religion and the sociology of recently settled communities. It is to this perspective that we now turn.

As scholars have considered both the biblical evidence and the kind of society that would have celebrated the festivals, they have come to the view that both of the harvest festivals—that is, the Harvest Festival of Deuteronomy 16:9–11 and the Festival of Shelters in Deuteronomy 16:13–15 (also called 'Ingathering', Exodus 23:16)—relate to an agrarian community, one that is settled enough to plant, grow and harvest crops. In the biblical texts, however, they are both related, one way or another, to the exodus and the desert wanderings, hence a nomadic background. The common understanding for these two contrasting features is that once the Israelites were settling in Canaan, they came across these harvest festivals in Canaanite customs and adapted them to their own faith journey. In a similar way, Easter (a spring festival) and Christmas (the winter solstice festival) were taken over and adapted for celebrating the Christian faith story.

Old Testament scholars go on to emphasize that this process should not be viewed as syncretism (accommodating Israel's faith to, say, Baal worship), because the festivals are now clearly dedicated to Yahweh. Furthermore, the demand that they should be celebrated at a central sanctuary was a way of ensuring that the festivals did not become contaminated by the practices of local pagan shrines or even social customs.

It is clear, then, that the harvest festivals imply a settled agricultural community. It could be argued that the Festival of 'Shelters' was a reminder of the time when the Israelites were nomads (Leviticus 23:43), but the shelters themselves were to be constructed from leafy branches cut from the people's trees (23:40), again implying a settled existence. The wandering people had lived in tents, not shelters made from branches, so at the very least there has been some accommodation to the new way of life.

A similar point can be made for the 'Thin Bread' aspect of the Passover. Here is how one German scholar puts it:

The original meaning of the rite seems to have been as follows. The farmers assemble in the sanctuaries in the cultivated land at the time of the barley harvest in order to enjoy the first new corn and the fresh loaves in a devout observance. Nothing leavened was permitted, for the new crops could not be mixed with the produce of the past year. Offerings to the deity, sacrifices and thanksgiving ceremonies were probably linked with the rite.[3]

We could also note that the entry into Canaan was not the first time, according to the biblical story, that the Israelites had been settled. They had, in fact, been settled for many years in Egypt. This might make it feasible that the 'settled' aspects of Harvest and Shelters could be accounted for by the time of Israel in Egypt. Against such a view we would have to set all the biblical material in Exodus to Deuteronomy which states clearly that these festivals were to be held on entry into the promised land. Israel did not look to pre-exodus events for their origins, and neither does Genesis tell us about the festivals.

Now, however, we recognize that there was communication between Egypt and Canaan for trade and military purposes while Israel was in Egypt. Also, the Old Testament indicates that Moses had spent many years outside Egypt and could have learnt about these kinds of festivals during those years. It is conceivable, therefore, that the instructions to adapt them for the settled life of the Israelites could have been formulated before they reached the promised land.

Whatever the exact history may have been, we should note the following:

• There are indications that Israel's three primary festivals have strong links to a settled, in contrast to a nomadic or semi-nomadic, society.
• Any 'pre-Israelite' or Canaanite elements, however, have been strongly subsumed within Israel's worship (the festivals are dedicated to

Yahweh), her faith story (they function as celebrations of that story as well as being agrarian festivals), and her society (the celebrations are held at a central location and all adult males attend). There is no suggestion of syncretism. Indeed, many features we have noted would act as a defence against syncretism.

- The Passover festival is positioned very differently, partly because it relates to animals that nomads can farm, but also because it is considered as part of the exodus events (Exodus 11—14) and is not simply ordained as a festival that in some way celebrates the origins of Israel and her faith.
- The process of adapting and giving new meaning to existing festivals is common (think of Easter and Christmas). In the case of the Passover it was realigned by Jesus as the Lord's supper. If we go back to our cathedral image, the fact that we can identify some stones as coming from a nearby castle does not mean that the cathedral functioned as a castle; indeed, the fact that the stones have been taken from the castle means that the castle ceased to function.
- If we want to appreciate what these festivals meant within Israel, we must pay close attention to what the Old Testament says about them rather than speculating about parallels with other societies; we should read them in the light of Israel's views, not impose general theories to help us understand them. Rarely, if anywhere, are we so well supplied with inside information on what rites and festivals may have meant for ancient societies as we are with Israel's. It is amazing how many accounts we have of how these festivals are to be carried out (in Exodus, Leviticus, Numbers and Deuteronomy), and these accounts need to be taken seriously in reaching a proper understanding of how the festivals operated and what their significance was.

As an illustration of all of this, we are now going to take a closer look at the third of the annual festivals: the Festival of Shelters.

THE FESTIVAL OF SHELTERS

So far, we have restricted ourselves to material found in the five Books of the Law. For all these festivals, however, there is other material too. In order to prepare us for our journey of exploration, let us note a very perplexing verse, namely Nehemiah 8:17. Here, following the reading of the law by Ezra, we learn that 'everyone who had returned from Babylonia built shelters. They lived in them and joyfully celebrated the Festival of Shelters *for the first time since the days of Joshua son of Nun* [my italics]'.

We are dealing here with a time after the Babylonian captivity and the return of the exiles to Judea, around 440BC. The reference to Joshua son of Nun looks back to around the twelfth century BC. The claim is, apparently, that for 750 years the Festival of Shelters has not been celebrated.

This seems to conflict with Ezra 3:4, which clearly comes before Nehemiah in the Bible: 'The people followed the rules for celebrating the Festival of Shelters and offered the proper sacrifices each day.' If we decide that Ezra's account relates to an event after the one described in Nehemiah (or perhaps the same event), we get rid of that particular clash, but we certainly don't deal with the wider issue.

We can also say that (as far as I am aware) there is no record of Shelters being celebrated in Joshua's time. That is not to say that it wasn't celebrated, of course, but why does Nehemiah 8:17 refer to him and not to Moses' instructions for the festival? What can be meant here?

One suggestion is that previously the *full* observance of the festival had been neglected. Derek Kidner thinks that 'the camping-out element had meanwhile lapsed or been reduced to a mere token... It seems to have been this aspect (a memorial of the wilderness) that had fallen into neglect'.[4] This is possible, but there is no strong evidence that this is what Nehemiah means, as far as I can see; it is, at best, a hypothesis worth considering.

Could Nehemiah mean that this was the first time the festival had been celebrated in the temple? This cannot be the case, as the rebuilding of the temple did not start until the following year. Anyway, people living in shelters did not require the temple, although the temple paraphernalia may have been required for sacrifices.

We should also note 2 Chronicles 8:13, which tells how Solomon, after the first temple had been built, 'followed the requirements that Moses had given for the sacrifices offered on the sabbath, on the first day of each month, the Festival of Thin Bread, the Harvest Festival, and the Festival of Shelters.' It is also worth looking at 1 Kings 8:1–2 and 65, which affirm that Shelters was celebrated when the temple was built:

Solomon decided to have the chest moved to the temple while everyone was in Jerusalem, celebrating the Festival of Shelters during Ethanim, the seventh month of the year... Solomon and the huge crowd celebrated the Festival of Shelters at the temple for seven days.

Perhaps, then, Nehemiah means that this was the first time that Shelters was celebrated (a) by those who were truly Israelite and so permitted to celebrate it, and (b) by all those others who were permitted to join in. It is certainly true that the legal texts stress the importance of all Israel gathering at a central place: Deuteronomy 16:13–15 clearly says that sons, daughters and servants are to be taken, as well as all the men, and Nehemiah 8 emphasizes their presence at the festival. Deuteronomy also says, however, that foreigners are to be invited, and there is no evidence in Ezra or Nehemiah that this was done—although Ezra may have thought it to be a wrong practice anyway.[5]

All we can really say is that we don't know.[6]

Nehemiah 8 does make a strong connection between Shelters and the reading of the Law (on the first day of the month) followed by national repentance, with shelters made from olive, myrtle and palm, and a daily ritual involving further teaching and reading from the law (see 8:13, 18). The day of confession, however, is on the 'twenty-fourth day' (Nehemiah 9:1–3). None of this quite fits with Leviticus 23:23–44, where the festival season begins with gathering at the sound of a trumpet on day one, the atonement festival including fasting on day ten, and Shelters on days 15–21.

What have we learnt by this closer look?

- The materials that we have suggest a very complex development process for the Festival of Shelters (and, by implication, for the other festivals), where variations may well have occurred between what was proposed in the law and what actually happened at any particular time.
- There appear to be differences in the various legal accounts, which may reflect different purposes in the laws, or different aspirations, or requirements at different times and in different contexts.
- It is difficult to pin down with any certainty what was thought to be the right way to do things. It may have varied for different groups of people within Israel.
- Shelters became associated not only with the time of wilderness wanderings but also with repentance, atonement and the reading of the

law. When there is a communal sense that people have disobeyed the law, the response of repentance then becomes understandable.

While our explorations show us that festivals were highly significant in Israel's life, we have to acknowledge that there are many gaps in our knowledge as to the precise details of how they were conducted.

The texts do provide reasons for keeping the festivals, both retrospective (linking to Israel's history) and prospective (God's promise of blessing for keeping them). The texts sometimes give great detail about the sacrifices that are part of the festivals, and this is important for a deeper understanding, but the legal texts do not give us many clues about what an ordinary Israelite may have thought of the festivals and their many constituent parts, or about the way people were encouraged to think and feel as their response to God. Is that because such individual or inward responses didn't matter? Looking at the legal texts might lead us to think so, but the appeals to the Israelites to celebrate and enjoy themselves in Nehemiah 8:9–12 show us that deeply felt personal responses and consequent changes of lifestyle were part of the reality of festivals too.

Passages such Nehemiah 8 alert us to the fact that there may be further Old Testament materials which could provide us with clues about the more personal significance of the festivals. As we will see later, the Psalms are a rich resource for this kind of understanding.

NOTES

1 'I'd rather you were faithful and knew me than offered sacrifices' is how the CEV puts it. This is strong but nevertheless rather predetermines the issue from our perspective.

2 Norman Snaith, *Mercy and Sacrifice* (SCM Press, 1953), pp. 100–101: 'Sacrifices are worse than useless if they are not backed by true living... In so far as sacrifices are the outward expression of true thankfulness of heart, they are acceptable to God.' And Walter Brueggemann, *Theology of the Old Testament* (Fortress, 1977), p. 678: 'A great deal of scholarly energy has gone into the question of whether these prophetic utterances oppose cult in principle, or oppose cult only when it is abusive and denies the reality of Yahweh. That scholarly conversation in the past was conducted in a context of extreme Protestant polemics against liturgical practices... In our present understandings, it is commonly judged that the prophets are concerned with the gross abuses in the cult and would not have entertained the notion of abolishing the cult.' Brueggemann then adds a footnote: 'See Amos 5:25; Jeremiah 7:22, for hints that some in Israel regarded sacrifice, in principle, as an aberration in Israel.'

3   H-J. Kraus, *Worship in Israel* (Blackwells, 1966), p. 48.

4   D. Kidner, *Ezra and Nehemiah* (IVP, 1979), p. 108.

5   See Ezra 10, where Ezra insists on the dissolution of marriages between Israelites and foreign women. It is worth adding, though, that in Nehemiah 9:2 we read, 'They refused to let foreigners join them, as they met to confess their sins.' This might imply that normally foreigners were allowed to join them; otherwise, why mention their exclusion here?

6   For those who are tempted to say, 'The solution is simple: the author of Nehemiah 8:17 was simply wrong', we have to question why the comment survived, or how the writer could apparently be so wrong, when there is a close connection between Chronicles and Nehemiah/Ezra. It is more feasible to reckon with the possibility that somehow we are missing the point.

PART THREE

WITHIN THE TEXT

Chapter 6

LIVING LAWS: THE OLD TESTAMENT AS TORAH

What comes to mind when you see the word 'law' in a biblical context? For many of us, our understanding of and emotional response to that word have been formed by two dominant forces. One is the way that the 'scribes and the Pharisees' (the upholders of 'law' in New Testament days) are presented in the Gospels. They are the people who are always picking on Jesus, trying to catch him out; they are the ones who put legal niceties before the needs of real people; they are the hypocrites, who say one thing and do another; they are those preeminently responsible for the crucifixion of Jesus. With this sort of perspective, it is not easy to read 'law' itself as something positive.

To this we add the common way of understanding 'law and gospel' in Paul, in passages like Romans 5:20–21 and Galatians 3:13, which states, 'But Christ rescued us from the Law's curse.' In such passages it is easy to think of 'law' as the antithesis of God's love, grace and gospel: those who promote or succumb to the 'law' are the enemies of the Christian faith. If this sort of view has influenced the way we approach Torah in the Old Testament, we are going to find it difficult to appreciate the high esteem with which law is treated there. But let's try!

THE VALUE OF TORAH

For a moment, reflect on the fact that the Torah, the law, makes up the first five books of the Bible. It is given pride of place in the biblical canon; by its position it is intended to shape the perspective we have on the whole Bible. It isn't, however, that these books describe the problem and the rest of the Bible provides God's solution, for these books also indicate God's solution and portray the first steps towards it. They provide the context for the whole drama: the creation of the universe, the fall, the call of Abraham and the covenant of grace with him, the birth of Israel in Egypt and the divine covenant with the chosen people. There are all kinds of laws, as we shall soon see, but these first five books (and the law they represent) are about life, not death.

Are there other examples that help us to adjust our perspective? Think, for instance, of the care in preparation and the excitement that accompanied the bringing of the ark of the covenant to Jerusalem under David's leadership; the point to remember here is that the ark was strongly linked to the Ten Commandments (see Exodus 25:16; Deuteronomy 10:1–5). The story tells us that David gathered 30,000 of Israel's best soldiers: 'David and the others were happy, and they danced for the Lord with all their might (2 Samuel 6:5). See the whole of 2 Samuel 6, and also 1 Chronicles 15—16.

Then we could drop in on King Josiah, when his attention has been drawn to 'The Book of God's Law' (2 Kings 22—23). Such was the impact on him that he initiated a root-and-branch process to remove any kind of compromise with pagan worship throughout the whole land, climaxing in a celebration of Passover: 'Josiah told the people of Judah, "Celebrate Passover in honour of the Lord your God..." This festival had not been celebrated in this way since kings ruled Israel and Judah' (2 Kings 23:21–22).

Fortunately, we can also gain an insider's perspective. The whole of Psalm 119 is essentially a eulogy for the law, or, more accurately, for the God who gave Israel the law. Here are a few verses that help us to catch the spirit with which the law could be regarded:

- 'Obeying your instructions brings as much happiness as being rich' (v. 14).
- 'Open my mind and let me discover the wonders of your Law' (v. 18).
- 'I love your commands! They bring me happiness. I love and respect them and will keep them in mind' (vv. 47–48).
- 'No matter where I am, your teachings fill me with songs' (v. 54).
- 'Our Lord, you are eternal! Your word will last as long as the heavens' (v. 89).
- 'Your teachings are sweeter than honey' (v. 103).
- 'Your word is a lamp that gives light wherever I walk' (v. 105).
- 'I praise you seven times a day because your laws are fair' (v. 164).

There are many more verses like this, in Psalm 119 alone. Together, they suggest a person who is besotted both with God and with the wonderful treasure of his law. This psalm cannot be considered simply as an emotional outburst. In fact, it is a most carefully constructed Hebrew poem, with each group of verses beginning with the same letter of the Hebrew alphabet, the groups being in alphabetical order and covering the whole alphabet. This conveys a sense of beautiful order being the perfect complement, as well as compliment, to the emotional and evocative language and the subject itself. This is what the law means—to a person who is not blind to the painful realities and perplexities of human life, for they too find ample expression within this litany of praise (see vv. 21–23, 86–87, 150).

The law, then, was not seen as a confining structure but as the life-giving and life-protecting gift of a gracious God for his people.

If this isn't enough to reorientate our vision of Torah, let me mention an encounter I had with a rabbi. He explained that, for him, as for all observant (that is, devout and practising) Jews, hearing the law being read is a very holy and significant experience. Fundamentally, it is not just listening to words; it is participating again in the first revelation of the law by God to Moses. It is a divine–human encounter, a personal meeting with God. This is the law, a wonderful gift of grace.

Leviticus 19

What is the law all about? The best answer, of course, would be to read it all and see for yourself. To gain a flavour of it, though, we can turn to Leviticus 19. Here we find many verses that are similar to the Ten Commandments. 'I am the Lord your God... Respect your father and your mother, honour the Sabbath... Do not steal or tell lies or cheat others' (vv. 1–4, 11). Such verses seem to be scattered throughout the passage.

In contrast to these succinct commands or prohibitions, there are details about when you can eat meat that has been sacrificed. There are also expressions of moral concerns: instructions to leave part of the harvest for the poor, not to mock people with disabilities, and to practise impartial justice. There is even the command to love others as much as you love yourself (vv. 9–10, 14–15, 18). Then, there are instructions about breeding animals and planting seeds, and a command not to wear garments of mixed cloth (v. 19). There are also prohibitions against eating blood, practising witchcraft and shaving your head (vv. 26–28).

In other words, there appear to be moral and ritual commands and prohibitions all mixed up together, with personal and public matters all treated as part of the same amalgam. It is extremely hard to find any explanation as to why the laws are put together in this order.[1] If we cannot explain the order, what can we make of it all?

Firstly, Israel's laws were concerned with every aspect of life, from sex to weights and measures, from farming to community building, from detailed religious practices to moral imperatives at the highest level.

Secondly, the way these laws are interwoven suggests that Israel saw her life as a whole. Religious practice, personal integrity, public justice, community behaviour and much more are all seen as under the sovereignty of God. Obedience in all of these aspects is part of what belonging to God means. In this respect, there is no apparent division between religious, political and personal behaviours.

Thirdly, we should note that laws that seem very strange to us, such as not wearing cloth made from two different materials, or not sowing two kinds of seed in the same field, may well have had very different implications for Israel. These particular laws were probably to do with prohibitions against some kinds of magic or controlling the supernatural powers; at least, that was how their pagan neighbours viewed these things, and Israelites were not to give any cause for their neighbours to think that they were drifting from their faith and community allegiance to Israel.

Fourthly, forgiveness is recognized as a necessary provision, and it is available. Verses 20–22 show this, and they also indicate the role of the priest in the process. What the verses do not make clear is how to understand this forgiveness: is it earned by the person who brings the sacrifice or is it all dependent on God's grace? A wider reading suggests that sacrifice is to be viewed in the latter way.

If we look carefully at the form of these laws, we can see that some are categorical and positive ('You must be holy', v. 1), some are categorical and negative ('Do not steal or tell lies or cheat others', v. 11), while others are conditional, somewhat like case laws. These laws develop on the basis of decisions that judges reach concerning very specific situations ('When you offer a sacrifice...', v. 5; If a man has sex with a slave woman...',

v. 20). Some people think that the categorical type originated in the context of worship while the conditional ones developed in the judicial system. Within the conditional type, however, there are also categorical commands!

Sixthly, there are some interesting 'motivations' given for keeping the laws. Positively, the people are to be holy because God is holy; and negatively, if they do unholy things they will cease to belong to God's community (vv. 1, 8). Again, positively, if they give the fourth year's fruit from a new tree to God, then in the fifth year it will produce 'an abundant harvest of fruit for you to eat' (v. 25); while negatively, if they let their daughters serve as temple prostitutes 'this would bring disgrace both to them and the land' (v. 29). The word 'disgrace' is a very interesting and powerful one. It should be associated with the more common word 'unclean'. If the land becomes unclean, then God warns of terrible consequences: 'the land will vomit them up'. This is also seen as a punishment of the land (Leviticus 18:24–30). Then there are historical motivations: the people are to treat foreigners well because they can remember what it was like to be foreigners in Egypt (v. 34).

Finally, we can note the overall framework given to these verses. Leviticus 19 begins, 'The Lord told Moses to say to the community of Israel…' (vv. 1–2), and ends with, 'I am the Lord your God. I rescued you from Egypt, and I command you to obey my laws' (vv. 36–37). In this way, these very varied words and laws are given divine status: they are spoken as if from God. Throughout their presentation, we are reminded of this through the use of first-person pronouns and adjectives referring to God: there are more than 20 such references. At the same time, the laws are presented as being mediated through Moses. A human voice, however, does not negate their divine origins.

What are we to make of the phrase 'the community of Israel' in verse 2? This grouping probably consists of all able-bodied males who are of a particular tribal origin or community status, although Leviticus 19 contains nothing explicit to exclude women of the right status. The people in this community are clearly involved in agricultural pursuits. They have a judicial system that depends on accurate human testimony, which, while it is vulnerable to bias, is intended to be scrupulously fair. Mention is made of slaves (who can be promised in marriage), foreigners, workers (presumably to be distinguished from the landowners), rich, poor, blind, deaf, children, old people and priests. It is noticeable that we hear nothing about 'the wise', or about craftsmen, soldiers, sailors, and political leaders, whom we meet elsewhere in the Old Testament. We do read about temple prostitutes and necromancers (people who claim they can talk to the dead). To what extent these different classifications are part of the 'community of Israel', and to what extent they are placed outside that community, is impossible to tell from these texts.

The final verses (vv. 36–37) are particularly significant and can shed some important light on the proper perspective for appreciating Israel's law. God claims to be their God, and the basis for his claim to their obedience to his laws is that he rescued them from Egypt. These verses seem to be a very succinct summary of many chapters in the book of Exodus, including the chapters that describe how the laws were first given in theophanic splendour (a theophany is a very vivid account of God making people aware of his presence) to Moses on Mount Sinai and, through him, to the community of Israel that God had delivered from Egypt (Exodus 19—20). These passages serve to remind Israel of the special relationship they have with their God, or, more precisely, that their God has with them.

In recent decades, scholars have noted a remarkable similarity between the kind of statement in Leviticus 19:36–37 and treaties between Hittite rulers and the groups of people to whom they related (roughly 14th–12th centuries BC). There was often a statement about the relationship, a reference to historical events of help, deliverance or generosity, and then a list of requirements to ensure that the people remained on good terms with and under the protection of the ruler. Often a primary requirement was that the people gave exclusive allegiance to this ruler, and rebellion was treated as a very serious offence. Such political arrangements seem to echo the covenant that God appears to have with his people. The nature of the historical relationship between these political treaties and Israel's covenant with God is likely to remain uncertain, but, at the very least, they provide a helpful analogy. This comparison reinforces our sense that Israel's laws were more than legal requirements. They were seen as a gift, helping her to remain in a privileged position in relationship to God, and enjoying his provisions and protection.

Our consideration of just one chapter of Leviticus has shown that the laws, or Torah, are both comprehensive and rich. They provide us with glimpses into Israel's society and her fundamental understanding of her relationship with God, the nature of community and the factors that could help to motivate the people to keep within the law. Law is seen as a gift from God through Moses to the community, but within the context of a historical process: it is not an abstract arrangement, like a constitution. We will consider the importance of this perceived historical process in the next chapter.

Of course, there are many other questions that we could ask about these laws. How were they preserved, by whom, and to whom were they read out and how frequently? Why were they preserved as they were, in all their variety but also with all their repetitions? To what extent were they observed, and were different laws of more significance at different times? Who was responsible for enforcing the laws or for determining punishments when people broke them (notice how little attention is given to this issue)? While we cannot hope to find answers to all these questions, we can investigate a little further by looking closely at a couple of groups of laws, beginning with those relating to the sabbath.

The sabbath

The most obvious place to begin when exploring the sabbath law in the Old Testament is within the Ten Commandments. The commandment relating to the sabbath can be found in two versions, Exodus 20:8–11 and Deuteronomy 5:12–15. The first point to note is the length of this command compared with most of the other nine, and the second is that it is the first of the two positive commands (the other being 'Respect your father and mother'). In a way, it acts as a bridge between the mainly religious demands about avoiding false worship and the more societal demands such as respect for parents,[2] and avoidance of murder and stealing. The bridge occurs in the concern for slaves and animals in the sabbath command: while sabbath observance is apparently a religious issue, there is a social aspect within it.

If we contrast the two accounts in Exodus and Deuteronomy, we can see that different motivations are given for observing the command. In Exodus, the reference is to creation and the fact that God ceased from his work on the seventh day (we recall the link to Genesis 2:1–3). In Deuteronomy, the reason given for sabbath-keeping is that the Israelites had been slaves in Egypt but God rescued them from slavery. This may seem an appropriate reason for including slaves in the sabbath remit, but not necessarily a reason for keeping it a 'holy day' (notice the different position of the reference to slavery in the two versions), so does Deuteronomy presuppose the more creational rationale as well? Or is it also implying that the sabbath, as well as the Passover, was a day for remembering the exodus?

What does it mean to keep something, particularly a day, holy? It would seem that it involves refraining from activities that are purely for our benefit, whether agriculturally or commercially. In this sense, it is still a negative command in content, even if it is positive in form: it means 'don't do work'. This is confirmed by Nehemiah 13:15–22, where Nehemiah prohibits work, particularly selling goods, on the sabbath and goes to considerable lengths to ensure that the people adhere to his edict. Incidentally, the steps he takes to ensure compliance also provide evidence that the sabbath law was not always applied rigorously.

Nehemiah gives us another insight, however. In chapter 8 we have the account of Ezra reading and explaining the law to all the people. They were deeply moved by this, weeping in repentance and remorse. Nehemiah and the other leaders with him said in response, 'This day is holy to the Lord your God, so you are not to mourn or cry. Now go home and have a feast. Share your food and wine with those who haven't enough. Today is holy to our Lord, so don't be sad' (vv. 9–10, GNB). Although this occasion is not specified as a sabbath day but as the first day of the seventh month, the procedures are reminiscent of the sabbath synagogue worship. In any case, it helps us to penetrate Israelite mentality about how you treat a day as 'holy'—not by remorse, silence and withdrawal but by partying and socializing. This rather contrasts with Exodus 35:2, which forbids even the lighting of a fire in the home, for cooking. Frequently, the sabbath is associated with solemn festivals and new moons, so the reference to the first day of the month may be further evidence that the day referred to in Nehemiah 8 was a sabbath.

In Exodus 31:12–17, we gain another perspective on the significance of the sabbath—as a sign of God's covenant: 'It is a sign between you and me for all time to come, to show that I, the Lord, have made you my own people' (GNB). Just as circumcision was given to Abraham as a sign of the covenant (Genesis 17:9–14), so the sabbath was given to Moses for the people. Again, there is a recollection of the exodus event, but now with more emphasis on the ongoing relationship between God and his people rather than, as with the Passover festival, on the initiatory event of deliverance from Egypt.

On several occasions, the high importance of keeping the sabbath is emphasized by the death penalty for those who break it, presumably because they are breaking the covenant and so putting the whole community at risk. Jeremiah 17:19–27 hints that the sabbath was not being properly observed and that defaulting on it was a breach of the covenant. Ezekiel 20 also indicates that the sabbath was highly important as a covenant sign and that its repeated breach was symptomatic of a much wider apostasy, thwarting God's gracious attempts to continue to work with Israel. The later chapters of Isaiah also echo this view, but in converse. Here we learn that even eunuchs or foreigners can find a place among God's people if they keep the sabbath properly (Isaiah 56:1–8). There is also the renewed promise of blessing for those who honour the sabbath, in Isaiah 58:13–14. Here, 'honouring' is equated with not pursuing your own interests and refraining from travelling, working, or talking idly.

From this survey we can gain the view that the sabbath was a special day, that the way it was 'kept holy' was expressed differently at different times, but that its core significance was to mark out the people of God as his own. It was a day that should benefit all who were associated with Israel, and can in this sense be seen as a 'promise', an indicator of the blessing God is seeking to bestow on all peoples.

Weights and measures

Amos 8:5 is an interesting verse, as it links the sabbath and commercial propriety. The prophet is critiquing the rich ruling classes in Samaria: 'You say to yourselves, "We can hardly wait for the holy days to be over so that we can sell our corn. When will the Sabbath end, so that we can start selling again? Then we can overcharge, use false measures, and tamper with the scales to cheat our customers"' (GNB).

Here the clear implication is that those who are barely managing to keep the Sabbath holy have not managed to keep just practices in their commerce. Evidence exists that merchants used one size of weights for buying and smaller ones for selling, thus increasing their profitability.[3] Micah 6:11 also condemns the use of false standards, while there is a whole section in Ezekiel seeking to establish what the true standards are for the future kingdom (45:9–12). What is remarkable here in Ezekiel is that these instructions are in the context of ensuring that the content of the sacrifices, such as grain and oil, were of the correct amount. Commerce, social justice and religious obligations intertwine.

The practice of falsifying weights and measures was forbidden in Israelite laws. Deuteronomy 25:13–16 states, 'Do not cheat when you use weights and measures. Use true and honest weights and measures, so that you may live a long time in the land that the Lord your God is giving you. The Lord hates people who cheat' (GNB).

We should note firstly that the motivation suggested for not cheating is the same as that for respecting parents (Exodus 20:12; Deuteronomy 5:16). By implication, not observing the command means that you have put yourself outside the covenant community and can no longer expect God's blessing and protection. Using honest weights was presumably regarded as being as fundamental to the preservation of Israelite society as was respecting parents (compare Leviticus 19:32–36, especially v. 35) Secondly, we see that God 'hates' those who fail to observe this law. This phrase occurs only in Deuteronomy (where, in 12:31 and 16:22, it relates to worshipping false gods) and Proverbs.[4] There has been some debate about whether one borrowed from the other, but they could well be independent uses.

In Proverbs, it is not only 'false weights' that God hates. He also 'hates' people who do evil, liars, evil-minded people, evil thoughts and biased judgments (Proverbs 3:32; 11:20; 12:22; 15:26 and 17:15; see also 6:16, which lists seven things that the Lord hates), but the law against false standards is reflected twice in Proverbs. For instance, in 20:10, 'The Lord hates people who use dishonest weights and measures' (GNB). In 11:1 we find, 'The Lord hates people who use dishonest scales. He is happy with honest weights' (GNB).

If we explore Proverbs 3:32–33, we can gain a clearer sense of what it means for the Lord to 'hate' something or someone. It actually means that he 'puts a curse on them' or 'has no use for them', meaning that he does not acknowledge and favour them. Thus, again, it looks rather as though such a person is beyond the protection that belongs to the covenant people.

With respect to false weights and measures, connections have been made to the Egyptian *Wisdom of Amenemope*, which could date from around the eighth to sixth centuries BC:

> *Do not lean on the scales nor falsify the weights,*
> *Nor damage the fractions of the measure…*
> *Make not for thyself weights that are deficient;*
> *They abound in grief through the will of the god (16).*[5]

This passage suggests too that the god Thot will protect the integrity of justice and fairness and punish those who seek to mislead others.

What we can see from this is that a law could be of primary concern for social practice but still have a very clear sanction from Yahweh. We can also glimpse how the Torah, the prophets and the wise could all have a legitimate interest in the application of a single type of law. Although such social laws may well be found in other cultures, the involvement of Yahweh changes the ethos of the law, because a breach of the law implies exclusion from the covenant, perhaps for the nation and not simply the individual.

Israel's laws form a very rich tapestry for her community. Far from being tedious obligations, they are the markers for a pathway that leads to the life of God's blessing. The prohibitions and restrictions mark out the dangerous territory, much as today we might warn people where landmines are to be found. The Torah is a gift, but it also becomes a yardstick by which prophets and wise men can call Israel to account.

NOTES

1 Biblical scholar Martin Noth writes, 'This codex is indeed remarkably diverse and disordered… it is understandable that it has been asked again and again whether a basic form, to some extent united in shape and substance, cannot be discerned.' Noth's conclusion is that no one has succeeded and that we would do better to concentrate on the content of individual laws. See *Leviticus* (SCM Old Testament Library, 1965), pp. 138–39).

2 Note that in Leviticus 19:3, both of these commands are reiterated, but the order is reversed: respecting parents comes before honouring the sabbath.

3 See J.L. Mays, *Amos* (SCM Press, 1969), p. 144: 'In the excavations at Tizrah shops were found dating to the eighth century which had two sets of weights, one for buying and one for selling.'

4 See W. McKane, *Proverbs* (SCM Press, 1970), p. 301.

5 Ed. J.B. Pritchard, *The Ancient Near East* (OUP, 1958), p. 241.

Chapter 7

ISRAEL AND THE IMPORTANCE OF HISTORICAL REMEMBRANCE

Is an appreciation of history a waste of time, or is it something that distinguishes humans from animals? Both views can be defended, but from a western European perspective, history is a discipline run on the lines of the Enlightenment model: only facts that can be verified by scientific methods, in particular the method of analogy, are accepted as having happened.

Almost inevitably this means that history is an account of human societies and their interactions. It may be political or royal; it may be about science or art, philosophy or technology; it may be about details or the 'big picture'; it may be a Marxist or a capitalist view; it may study social movements or the impact of significant individuals; but its farthest horizon is what *human beings* have thought, said, done and sought to control. Ultimately it is about us, and as such it helps us, either intentionally or indirectly, to understand (or at least to understand why we cannot understand) who we are, how we got to where we are, who the 'other' is and why we understand and relate to others in the way that we do. While history may vary in myriad ways as to subject-matter and method, in some way or another its basic materials are located in the past, and it appeals to them for the justification of any claims it makes.

We have mentioned already in several contexts that the Old Testament appears to be related to history. It can be located within a historical and political framework, it presents itself as a historical story, it can be investigated with many of the tools and methodologies of the historian, and it often refers to Israel's history for making claims and bringing challenges.

HISTORY—HUMAN AND DIVINE

Over time, however, people have come to recognize that there is a fundamental divide between the history that the Old Testament presents to us and the approach to history that is accepted as 'proper' in our culture. While the ultimate horizons of our history are human (it forms part of the Enlightenment 'human reason alone' approach), the ultimate horizon of the Old Testament is God. If we are part of the Christian faith community, it is easy to overlook this foundational difference. As we read secular history, we may carry our faith presuppositions into that reading; so we may think we discern that, in the long term, acting justly is more significant than holding power, or even that factors surrounding Hitler's plans to invade Britain—such as the deterioration of the weather—were God's response to people's prayers. Equally, we carry (in varying degrees) our secular perspectives and critiques into our reading of the Old Testament.

In the end, recognizing that the 'plausibility structures' (the fact that we have to decide what could or could not have happened in the past on the basis of what we think is possible) of these two approaches is different has led scholars to talk about Israel's own way of seeing history (which could be nearly as varied as our own but in different ways) as 'salvation history'. The attempt has been made to understand what Israel's history looked like to her, and why and how it all worked, so that we do not overlay and distort her understanding with our secularly biased approaches. Having done this, there are some scholars who want to make the next move and let these two 'plausibility structures' engage with one another: in other words, to allow for the possibility that, when the Bible speaks of God rescuing Israel from Egypt, in some way he was the cause for this deliverance. Perhaps human reason and actions alone cannot claim to give us the whole of reality. This endeavour is not an abstruse theological exercise: it has the potential to challenge the fabric of our society—about, for example, the assumption of the absoluteness of the profit motive, or the view that death should be avoided at all costs—just as Einstein's theory of relativity reshaped science.

EXODUS

Our priority in this chapter, though, is to gain some sense of what 'history' meant to Israel. In a moment, we will look at some of her historical texts. Before we do, take a moment to jot down what you recall as the key features of Israel's 'Exodus from Egypt'. Having compiled your list, give each feature a letter: a, b, c, d and so on.

Now consider the passages below and match the number of each passage with a feature on your list. So, for instance, if you remembered 'slavery', this will be marked against readings 1 and 2 (and possibly 6 and 7, because these two passages hint at severe difficulties without specifying slavery). If you wrote down 'rescued from Egypt', then you will note 1, 4 and 8. You might want to ask yourself what you had in mind when you wrote 'rescue'—release from slavery or the Red Sea episode, or both.

1 I am the Lord your God, the one who brought you out of Egypt where you were slaves (Exodus 20:2).

2 The Egyptians were cruel and had no pity on us. They ill-treated our people and forced us into slavery. We called out for help to you, the Lord God of our ancestors. You heard our cries; you knew we were in trouble and abused. Then you terrified the Egyptians with your mighty miracles and rescued us from Egypt (Deuteronomy 26:6–8).

3 When Israel was a child, I loved him, and I called my son out of Egypt. But as the saying goes, 'The more they were called, the more they rebelled.' … I took Israel by the arm and taught them to walk (Hosea 11:1–3).

4 People of Israel, I rescued you from Egypt. Now listen to my judgment against you. Of all nations on earth, you are the only one I have chosen. That's why I will punish you because of your sins (Amos 3:1–2).

5 Our God has said: 'Encourage my people! Give them comfort. Speak kindly to Jerusalem and announce: Your slavery is past; your punishment is over. I, the Lord, made you pay double for your sins.' Someone is shouting: 'Clear a path in the desert!' (Isaiah 40:1–3).

6 When our ancestors were in Egypt, you saw their sufferings; when they were at the Red Sea, you heard their cry for help. You knew that the King of Egypt and his officials and his nation had ill-treated your people. So you worked fearsome miracles against the Egyptians and earned a reputation that still remains (Nehemiah 9:9–10).

7 They were the Lord's people, so he let them grow stronger than their enemies. They served the Lord, and he made the Egyptians plan hateful things against them. God sent his servant Moses. He also chose and sent Aaron to his people in Egypt, and they worked miracles and wonders there. Moses and Aaron obeyed God, and he sent darkness to cover Egypt (Psalm 105:23–28).

8 When they were in Egypt, they paid no attention to your marvellous deeds or your wonderful love. And they turned against you at the Red Sea. But you were true to your name, and you rescued them to prove how mighty you are. You said to the Red Sea, 'Dry up!' Then you led your people across on land as dry as a desert. You saved all of them and drowned every one of their enemies. Then your people trusted you and sang your praises (Psalm 106:7–12).

This very simple exercise will have shown up two facts about even this small selection of passages: firstly, that there are many and varied details that go to make up our full remembered picture of the exodus; and secondly, that there are different degrees of detail. General terms, such as 'severe difficulties' or 'rescue', have the advantage that they allow us to fill them with our concepts; they have the disadvantage that when we use them we may be referring to more than one thing in the biblical accounts, or even completely different realities from what was originally meant. For instance, we could be referring to the release from Egypt and slavery as 'salvation', but we might have in our minds a Christian view such as 'salvation from sin'.

Now have another look at the passages, noting even more variety and also the precision, or lack of it, that is used. You may also want to add to your original list any factors that you omitted.

Let us now turn to some of the other features of these passages. Sometimes a passage has God speaking to Israel (1); sometimes it has 'Israel' speaking to God (8). Sometimes it is in a reporting mode (7);

sometimes, even when God speaks, he is recounting to a third party (3). When Israel is speaking, sometimes the verses use 'them' for the Israelites in Egypt (8) and sometimes 'we' (2). Each of these ways of speaking probably reflects a different function in Israel's life and worship, such as using the words as a sort of creed, or to justify behaviour, or as a response to God's goodness in worship.

Sometimes the passage is used to stress Israel's privilege, and sometimes its responsibilities. Sometimes God's goodness is used as a motive for obedience, sometimes as the grounds for judgment (compare 1 and 4).

Not only does the intensity of detail vary, but so also does the timespan being described. It can be as short as the moment of release from slavery, but it can include the wilderness wanderings as well as the Red Sea episode (compare 1 and 8). It may begin in Egypt at the time of rescue, or recount why Israel needed rescuing. It may even explain how Israel came to be in Egypt (7).

Usually, in these passages, the only observable participants are God, Israel and the Egyptians, although Moses and Aaron appear in number 7. There are a variety of theological nuances carried in these texts. For example, God may take the initiative or he may act in response to Israel's appeals for help (compare 7 and 6). He may act because he has chosen them, or even though they are rebellious (4 and 8). Perhaps these nuances reflect the different situations of the people for whom the texts were being used.

It is worth reading these passages in their biblical contexts to see the bigger picture in which they appear, or finding other similar passages and considering how they reflect some of the issues we have highlighted.

One of the many fascinating questions to ask is to what extent the mention of 'rescue from Egypt' would haave triggered an individual Israelite's recollection of the whole story from Joseph bringing Jacob and his brothers to settle in Egypt, including the numerical growth of the people and the Egyptians' opposition to them, the years of hardship, the life of Moses, the confrontation between Moses (and Aaron) and Pharaoh, the many miracles that led to Israel's release, the crossing of the Red Sea, the wanderings in the wilderness, the rebellions, and so on. If we cannot assume that everyone had access to the whole story as recounted in the Torah, then we cannot be sure how comprehensive most people's recollections would have been. In trying to understand what any specific passage would mean, we have to be careful not to import our own recollections into the passage, based on our own broad knowledge of the scriptures. Equally, we cannot assume that because there is no reference to Moses in a particular, he would not have been in people's minds when they wrote, said or heard these words.

One way scholars have worked with the exodus experience is to suggest that an originally simple recounting, like our passage 1, acted like a magnet to which all kinds of other stories were gradually added, until the full story emerged as recounted in Exodus and related books. It is equally conceivable that the process worked the other way round: at times when the whole story was well known, it was possible to use a kind of narrative shorthand and have the same impact. In other words, the whole recollection could be triggered by a few words. A parallel in our context would be a reference to the prodigal son: you only need to tell the whole story if your audience do not know their Bibles or if, knowing that they are very familiar with the story and a specific understanding of it, you want to change that understanding.

What becomes clear is that Israel made use of the experience of slavery and rescue from Egypt by God in many different contexts (law, worship, prophecy, historical recounting) and at many different times in her history (take Amos and Nehemiah as illustrations). Engaging with this remembered experience was a fundamental way in which Israel understood herself, her present situation, her relationship with God and indeed what God himself was like. It was often through this series of events that she found direction for her future and the resolve to live well, often in difficult circumstances.

While it is notable that this remembered experience travelled with her as she settled in the promised land, became a nation with a king, struggled with superpower aggression, experienced defeat and exile, and eventually returned to her homeland, it is equally important to note how flexible were the ways she understood and applied the experience. It provided her with raw materials from which she could construct all kinds of different artefacts, so to speak; some were functional and some were 'luxury goods', but the fact that they were made from this raw material gave them legitimacy, and in the process added to the richness of all that the exodus meant to her. These events were foundational not only in that Israel looked back to them as the beginning of her own identity and purpose as the people of Yahweh, but also in the ongoing sense that they continued to shape her life and self-understanding.

THE BIGGER PICTURE

In looking at some snapshots of how Israel made use of the stories relating to the deliverance from Egypt, we have already noted many other aspects of her journey through more than a thousand years of history. Most of this material also became integrated into her own account of her story .

If we look again at Psalms 105 and 106, we can note a few stages on this pilgrimage. Psalm 105 incorporates references to the patriarchs (vv. 6, 12–18) and concludes with a brief reference to God giving Israel the land (v. 44). Psalm 106 pays more attention to the rebellion in the wilderness but gives some indication of the settlement in Canaan (vv. 34–39) and probably refers to exile (vv. 40–46) although we cannot be sure whether these verses refer to the northern defeat (exile from Samaria) or the southern (exile from Jerusalem). The psalm concludes with a request that God will 'bring us back from among the nations' (v. 47).

Between them, these two psalms relate stories from, or hint at, almost the whole of what we recollect as Israel's history. Clearly, each psalm has its own tone and purpose but between them they cover the events of a thousand years and more:

• The patriarchs
• Israel in Egypt
• Deliverance from Egypt
• Wilderness wanderings and disobedience
• Entrance to and settlement in the promised land
• A period of conquest by and deliverance from other nations
• The exile and the need for further deliverance

There are two interesting and somewhat striking omissions in these two psalms compared with the narratives from the records as we have them in the Torah and 1 Samuel—2 Chronicles (the books that give us Israel's history in detail). Firstly, there is no reference to God's revelation of his laws at Sinai, and secondly, there is no record of the kings of Israel and the significant part they played for good and ill over several hundred years.

Of course, Psalm 105:45 refers to obeying God's laws, but this is not the same as the historical accounts in, say, Exodus. Other Psalms contain such references or hints, although it is probably easier to find them for the kings of Israel, especially King David (see, for example, Psalm 89).

We should probably not make too much of these apparent omissions. After all, there are references to the kings in the prophetic books and plenty of reference to the law in much of the rest of the Old Testament. It may well be that the omissions in the Psalms are best accounted for by the festivals in which they were used (where the reading of the law would follow, and the ceremony itself provided a powerful reminder of the events at Sinai).

It is also clear both from many of the Psalms and from some of the prophets, such as Isaiah, that the theme of 'Zion'—the city of God—was very potent too. It would be possible for us to show how Zion functioned in a parallel way to the exodus for Israel, associated as it was with God's choice of David and his descendants as king, with the powerful sense of God's presence associated with the temple and its worship and with the promise of divine protection and delivery from enemies. Zion/Jerusalem can also be used positively and negatively, as a reason for praise and appeal for rescue, and can serve the prophets as an image in constructing their expectations for the future.

The image of Zion does not link so strongly to the story of God and his people as to the theme of God and king/city/temple. It does connect to some extent with the patriarchs, Abraham and Jacob especially. In Genesis 14:17–24 there is even a story linking Abraham to Jerusalem in a special way, in which Abraham pays tithes to the mysterious priest-king, Melchizedek. Nevertheless, although the kings and Jerusalem are clearly vital for the way Israel understood herself, her history and God, they do not appear to be quite so fundamental to the nation's identity as the exodus events.

As we have done with the exodus, it is possible to take many facets of Israel's history and see how those episodes have influenced the telling of other parts of her story. We can see how Israel worked out her life and faith in the light of key happenings, which provided a way of shaping and understanding contemporary events.

By now it should be becoming clear that, although in one sense we can easily retell the history of Israel from the accounts we have from the patriarchs, through the exodus and the conquest to the exile and later developments, in another sense this is, even from the inner perspective of the Old Testament, only part of the story. We have seen how different people at different times will make use of different parts of this story, either by focusing exclusively on their selected episode, or by the weight of attention given to different parts. We have noted how the same events may be used in many ways, by reshaping and reapplying the stories, casting them in different lights. We have all kinds of ways of telling the story, from one-liners to whole books. What is clear, though, is that on many occasions Israel's storytellers, priests and prophets sought to understand what was happening to her because of her relationship with God, and how she ought to respond, by allowing her primary historical experiences to cast not so much their shadow as their light on to the present.

Chapter 8

DYNAMIC VOICES: THE CONTRIBUTION OF THE PROPHETS

We have already referred to the prophets a number of times. This is entirely appropriate because the prophets were not ethereal people who lived in some mysterious stratosphere removed from ordinary mortals. Rather, they were people who lived in everyday, ordinary places as well as at the centre of political activity, involved in the maelstrom of events. They formed their words and performed their deeds in the specific contexts of their lives; they were not celestial stargazers or remote philosophers untouched by the people, movements and happenings around them.

Nevertheless, it is proper that we also pay them—and more especially their messages—particular attention. At one time in the history of Old Testament interpretation, such a statement would have been based on their significance as foretellers of Jesus; at a later date, it would probably have been made because they represented the highest standards of religion and ethics in the Old Testament, still later because they were key social reformers. These justifications reflect the particular standpoint of those making the claims rather than an accurate perspective derived from the Old Testament. We should give the prophets particular attention because the Old Testament itself presents them as being worthy of attention.

If we mention 'Old Testament prophets', what is likely to come to mind is one of the great prophetic books of Isaiah, Jeremiah or Ezekiel, or the courageous, epoch-making pages of Amos or another of the twelve 'minor prophets', but we should also remember that the books we regard as historical are known in the Hebrew Bible as the 'former prophets'. This surprises us, because they seem simply to tell the story of Israel's development and demise, the prime focus being on the founding of the monarchy, with Saul, David and Solomon and successive kings of various types. How often, in the 'historical' books, do we come across passages such as: 'Abijam did not truly obey the Lord his God as his ancestor David had done. Instead, he was sinful just like his father Rehoboam… Asa obeyed the Lord, as David had done... As long as Asa lived, he was completely faithful to the Lord' (1 Kings 15:3, 11, 14). Such assessments imply that Israel's future was largely determined by the behaviour of its kings. The significance of the kings is even more notable through the recurrent phrase that 'everything else that X did while he was king is written in *The History of the Kings of Israel*'; this was presumably a resource book well known to Israelite readers, which indicates that there was much more to tell about the monarchs than found its way into our versions.

Nevertheless, all this history is presented to us as the work of the 'former prophets'. One perceptive scholar has suggested that the prophets' words were like the gears of a car: it was through their words that history moved on, and without them Israel's history wouldn't have happened.

PRELIMINARY STUDY

Before we look at some aspects of the prophets' message, we have two preliminary tasks. The first is to acquaint ourselves with the variety of material that we have about the prophets. The Old Testament contains a wide range of presentations, varying from brief episodes on prophets about whom we know hardly anything (see, for instance, 1 Kings 13, where there are two unnamed prophets) to spans of several chapters, including many different kinds of stories, the most notable being the many episodes in the lives of Elijah and his successor, Elisha (1 Kings 17 to 2 Kings 13). Here, also, we come across the 'sons of the prophets'—presumably something like disciples, bands of prophets or a prophetic movement—but we have no real way of knowing how stable, in terms of membership, such groups were.

Sometimes, within the prophetic books themselves, we have stories about the prophets too, particularly Jeremiah (see Jeremiah 18—19; 36), but also Isaiah (see Isaiah 7; 36—38). Even with Hosea this is probably the case: although the CEV translates Hosea 1 as if it is a first-person narrative, most translations (see GNB and NIV, for instance) recognize that the chapter is a third-person narrative. Whereas the stories about Isaiah also occur in Kings and some in Chronicles as well (compare Isaiah 36—38 with 2 Kings 18—20 and 2 Chronicles 32), in Hosea they only appear in the book bearing his name and are hard to reconcile with the material from Hosea himself, because there seem to be several contradictions (see Hosea 1 and 2, for instance).

In some of these stories, the emphasis is on what happens—the events and, in particular, what happens to the people referred to (whether individuals or groups). In others, the emphasis is on the message that the prophet delivers. The latter case represents a halfway house between stories about the prophets and collections of oracles where the words of the message are the normal focus. These collections of oracles can be so detached from any historical anchorage that we often struggle to reconstruct the original context that prompted the message. To illustrate these processes, we can consider a chapter in Isaiah. In Isaiah 7:1–9, although there is a clear context provided, the emphasis is on the message; in Isaiah 7:10–17 the message moves more to the forefront, although there is a scanty context provided in verse 10. Then, with the collection of oracles beginning 'When that time comes' (7:18, 20, 21, 23, GNB), we are given no clues to the context: it seems likely that these oracles were brought together simply because of the way they begin. Now the message has become the absolute focus.

Our second preliminary task is to ask how we can account for the variety of story-like materials. The simple explanation is that it is a straightforward indication of the original situations where the prophecies or prophetic actions took place. Other factors almost certainly come into play, though, such as who was around to tell the stories and then preserve them in writing. We need to consider what aspects of prophecy really interested these people, for this may have influenced which materials were more highly valued and therefore more likely to be communicated to the people at the time, as well as being preserved for posterity. In the case of Jeremiah, we do have some indications of how and why certain materials were kept (see Jeremiah 36). There are also other clues in Isaiah 8:16–18, but we cannot use these clues to reconstruct general principles because we do not know whether the accounts are there by chance, or because they are illustrative of generalities, or because they stood out against the known norms for writing down prophetic messages.

These factors, among others, show us that it is rather difficult to construct a 'lives of the prophets' or 'prophetic personalities' kind of book that would satisfy a thirst for cult hero biographies or film, or even one that would provide the basis for sermons aiming to engage listeners with the prophets through their 'common humanity'. This is not to dismiss such constructions entirely, partly because in some of the biblical material there is a fascination with the prophets and even their personalities, and also because, when it is done astutely, this approach can engage us long enough to enable us to absorb some of the prophets' message. We do need to be aware, however, of the limitations in our sources for this task.

The positive side to this warning is that it alerts us to ask what the prophetic material is really seeking to accomplish, and how it impacts us today. To take one example, Amos 1—2 is apparently a series of oracles pronouncing God's judgment on the chief foreign cities and small nations that surrounded Israel, such as Damascus, Philistia and even Judah. The real purpose, though, is to emphasize the seriousness of Israel's sin and the inevitability of divine judgment on the nation (remember that, by now, the nation was split into Judah and Israel).

This might then raise the question of whether the oracles of doom found towards the end of Jeremiah and other prophets have their place in the Old Testament as violent condemnations by God, or whether they too serve another purpose. It has been suggested that the prophetic books of Isaiah, Jeremiah and Ezekiel are structured basically as (a) condemnation of Israel; (b) condemnation of the nations; (c) salvation of Israel; (d) salvation of the nations—with the overall message that God's purposes are to bring salvation to all, but that the pathway must include making people aware of the seriousness of their transgressions. Such an understanding should have an impact on the way we use these individual passages today: to use the oracles that condemn the nations as though their message is ultimately about God's punishment would not reflect their place in the bigger picture of ultimate salvation.

The bulk of what we regard as prophetic materials are collections of the prophets' oracles or pronouncements. As we have already seen, much of this material is undated and the context is not very specific (see, for another illustration, Isaiah 1). A significant but minor amount does provide some background (consider Isaiah 6:1; 7:1–3). There is even, occasionally, material that is attributed to more than one prophet (see Isaiah 2:2–4; Micah 4:1–3; but note also the differences in the surrounding words). Many scholars think, particularly in relation to Isaiah, Jeremiah and Ezekiel, the so-called 'major prophets', that the collection of their oracles acted like a magnet, drawing other known oracles towards them, which attracted still further material, thus leading to the large collections we now have. To us, this might seem like deception, but the legal concept of copyright and authorship did not exist in Old Testament times. Perhaps a better way to view it is that such accumulations of materials indicate the prestige in which these three great prophets were held: the materials that were added were understood to demonstrate not only the impact of their ministries on other prophets but also the outworking of the prophetic words, so the new materials should properly be attributed to their sources. Any analysis of what was original and what might have been added is necessarily speculative, however. We need to be aware of this, as well as the fact that such an understanding does not have to detract from the value of the material as scripture.

Other prophets

The prophets we meet either through stories about them or through their collections of oracles are not the only ones about whom we have some insight. There are also the 'false prophets'. Going right back to the first prophet for whom we have a collection, Amos, we find him apparently rejecting the claim that he is a prophet (Amos 7:12–15).[1] It would seem that, for Amos, being described as a prophet was something of an insult, and yet for us his words are the epitome of what a prophet's message should be.

Any simple distinction between the real and the false prophets is hard to make. Were the false prophets those that worked in the temple? Were they paid to deliver their messages? Was the source of their inspiration false, or at least superficial, in that they constructed their own prophecies? Did their messages not come true? Were they considered false because they prophesied hope? Or did the prophets' 'falsehood' consist in their immoral and apostate behaviour? These and other features can be discerned as criteria that the biblical prophets applied in their attempt to discriminate the faithful prophet of Yahweh from those whose messages were false. Here are some key verses to consider.

Some day a prophet may come along who is able to perform miracles or tell what will happen in the future. Then the prophet may say, 'Let's start worshipping some new gods…' If the prophet says this, don't listen!
DEUTERONOMY 13:1–3

'How can we tell if a prophet's message really comes from the Lord?' You will know, because if the Lord says something will happen, it will happen. And if it doesn't, you will know that the prophet was falsely claiming to speak for the Lord.

DEUTERONOMY 18:21–22

A spirit came forward and said to the Lord, 'I can trick Ahab.'
   'How?' the Lord asked.
   'I'll make Ahab's prophets lie to him.'

1 KINGS 22:21–22

You prophets and priests think so little of me, the Lord, that you even sin in my own temple! … The prophets in Samaria were disgusting to me, because they preached in the name of Baal and led my people astray. And you prophets in Jerusalem are even worse. You're unfaithful in marriage and never tell the truth. You even lead others to sin instead of helping them turn back to me… Don't listen to the lies of these false prophets, you people of Judah! The message they preach is something they imagined; it did not come from me… The prophets tell them, 'The Lord has promised everything will be fine.' But I, the Lord, tell you that these prophets have never attended a meeting of my council in heaven or heard me speak. They are evil!

JEREMIAH 23:11, 13–14, 16–19

Those lying prophets are doomed! They don't see visions… They don't warn the people about coming trouble… Those prophets lie by claiming they speak for me, but I have not even chosen them to be my prophets. And they still think their words will come true… they are full of lies.

EZEKIEL 13:3, 5–7

One biblical scholar has tried to summarize this very complex issue as follows.

The marks by which one could recognize a true or a false prophet cannot be expressed in a formula… Different features had to be taken into consideration… The general agreement of a prophet's preaching with Yahweh's will, thoughts and purposes guaranteed the fact that this prophet had been sent by Yahweh and had a true divine message to convey.[2]

In addition to the false prophets, there are what we could call the 'hidden prophets'. Occasionally in the historical books we come across prophetic announcements that are not attributed to anyone actually called a prophet. An illustration of this is the message of Jehu, son of Hanani, to King Baasha (see 1 Kings 16:1–7). It is also likely that we have some prophetic sayings within the Psalms: much of Psalm 50 could be a 'prophetic utterance'. There is much support for the view that the phenomenon known as 'change of mood' (where someone is lamenting their dreadful plight and anxieties one instant, and the next is suddenly full of confidence and praise for God) comes about when the psalmist receives a message from a prophet who works within the temple environment (see Psalm 22:21 compared to v. 22; and Psalm 30:10 compared to v. 11). In some Psalms we can even hear the message that is given—for instance, in Psalms 32:8 and 60:6. In Isaiah 38, also, we can see the impact of the prophet's message on King Hezekiah, with the prophet's message in verses 4–6 and the 'change of mood' registered in Hezekiah's words between verses 15 and 16.

Finally, there is material that attributes the title or role of prophet to a person, such as Moses, and allows us to see how prophets were regarded at the time: 'I am going to let your brother Aaron speak for you. He will tell your message to the king, just as a prophet speaks my message to the people' (Exodus 7:1; compare Deuteronomy 18:15–19).

The Bible provides us with a huge range of materials relating to prophecy, so what is the true nature of prophecy? What made a person identifiable as a prophet? Various answers have been proposed to these questions, sometimes on the basis of etymology (so the word 'seer' may be interpreted by some scholars as implying that a prophet had to receive his message through visual images), sometimes on the basis of comparative studies with similar religious phenomena in other ancient Near Eastern cultures (such as ecstasy—strange behaviours attributed to the gods having taken possession of the person).

But a strong case can be made, however, for understanding the prophets as messengers of Yahweh, partly on the basis of their own self-understanding ('Yahweh does nothing without revealing it to his servants the prophets', Amos 3:7; Isaiah 6; Jeremiah 1), partly on the basis of analysing a common rhetorical form used by the prophets, which is known as the 'messenger formula'.[3] We can also note the sociological origin of the prophets within the kingdom (as messengers between rulers), which concurs with the understanding of Yahweh's relation to Israel as that of Lord to covenant vassal (the vassal being the nation in subjection to or protected by the Lord). Messengers had a critical role to play by delivering warnings to the vassal people about the dangers of breaching the covenant, then announcing the coming judgment and sometimes offering to restore the relationship. This understanding also helps us appreciate the complementary role of the prophets as Israel's intercessors: people who carry messages back to the overlord on behalf of the vassals.

While we must clearly recognize that changes in social and political context, as well as the individual circumstances and even personality of any prophet, are all going to modify what counts as prophecy, seeing the prophets as Yahweh's messengers to his people (and to the king as the chief representative of the people) does provide a genuinely helpful and unifying starting-point.

MESSENGERS OF GOD

We have seen that prophecy is a wide-ranging phenomenon in the Old Testament, but a central clue to understanding at least the prophets who are identified as such in the Bible is to view them as messengers of God, the covenant Lord, to his (disobedient) vassal people. When the prophets do address an individual, it is usually a ruler who carries responsibility for his people.

We now turn to consider a few key themes in relation to five of the prophets, namely Amos, Hosea, Isaiah, Jeremiah and Ezekiel.

The prophets believed they were called directly by God, and re-counting this call is significant for the written text as well. Amos 7:14–15 is highly suggestive here: 'I'm not a prophet! And I wasn't trained to be a prophet. I am a shepherd, and I take care of fig trees. But the Lord told me to leave my herds and preach to the people of Israel.' We can see from the context that he was speaking in a confrontational situation, where Amaziah, the priest at the king's temple in Bethel, was seeking to silence Amos even as he was establishing his right to speak. We can also see that Amos had been carrying out an ordinary role in society before his call came: he was not part of the religious or social establishment. Finally, we can note that the reason Amaziah wanted to silence Amos was that his words were considered dangerous to the king (vv. 10–11), perhaps because they were likely to stir up rebellion, but more probably because of the inherent power of the prophetic word.

For Hosea, his call was integral to his relationship with his wife, but the details remain obscure (chs. 1—2). For Isaiah, it was connected with an experience in the temple, apparently within the context of worship (ch. 6). Jeremiah's call came to him as a youth, but exactly how and where we do not know (1:4–7). For Ezekiel, who was from a priestly family, a powerful visionary experience marked his call (chs. 2—3). These call accounts were probably used by those who supported and followed the prophets, as well as in confrontational situations between the prophets and those who wanted to neutralize their claims to speak for God. They certainly indicate that the prophets were distinctive (Moses, Samuel, David and Solomon are reported as having similar encounters with God), and their 'direct line' to God appears to be one strong reason why the prophets were taken so seriously.

What was at the heart of their messages? We need to understand that these prophets were speaking to very specific situations, so the content of their messages varies enormously. This variety is also, of course, indicative of the fact that they were different personalities with different intellectual and religious resources to draw on in order to communicate their messages. Nevertheless, there are some core themes that do recur.

- Israel's relationship with God requires people to behave in appropriate ways to other members of their community (irrespective of their social status). So Amos speaks of social justice (5:10–15), Hosea of covenant mercy (4:1–3), Isaiah of righteousness (1:21–28), Jeremiah of falsehood and broken promises (5:1–5) and Ezekiel of murder and violence (7:23). The prophets were alert observers and were unafraid when it came to critiquing their society and their leaders. They did so from the security of their own standing before God, and appear to have gained their evaluation of society by understanding the traditions of God's rescue of his people and his provision of laws by which they should live. Echoes of these laws, as exemplified in the Ten Commandments, recur in the prophets' oracles.
- Fundamentally, however, the issue is that Israel has broken her relationship with God. The waywardness of the nation's worship is demonstrated by the way they have become involved with Baalism

(Hosea), and by their involvement with and submission to foreign superpowers (Isaiah). They place false trust in the temple and its rituals (Jeremiah), while polluting their worship in the temple by improper performances and bringing in traces of other religions (Ezekiel). Behind all of these factors, though, the fundamental charge is Israel's rebellion against God.

- The prophets place emphasis on the amazing qualities of God. Hosea focuses on his astonishingly committed and caring love, Amos majors on his righteousness linked to his universal rule over all nations, and Isaiah on his transcendent holiness. Jeremiah's focus is on God's sovereign power and Ezekiel's is on his glory and power.
- Beyond the brokenness of the relationship with God, all these prophets look towards a process of restoration. Hosea follows through on his marriage experience and looks to God to woo Israel again, whereas Amos speaks of a new ruler. Isaiah has many images, but again the divinely chosen and equipped ruler is a central motif, linked to miraculous deliverance. For Jeremiah, the concept of a new (meaning 'of a different order') covenant is a powerful force. In Ezekiel, it is the restored temple that dominates his future hope. In connection with this process of restoration, we should note that many scholars think that at least some of these powerful images of hope were added later, and may not even originate with the prophets themselves. Nevertheless, reading them in the context of the Old Testament, we can see them as part of the prophetic message.

Biblical prophecy is, then, a very rich phenomenon: in fact, probably the plural 'phenomena' is more appropriate! What we can discern is that prophets were people who stood out from the crowd—although some-times they had followers, and indeed someone had to preserve their sayings. They considered themselves summoned by Yahweh into his intimate council (see Jeremiah 23:18; 1 Kings 22:19; Isaiah 6:1–3) and authorized to deliver his message. Often this message critiqued the *status quo*, and particularly challenged those in authority, whether kings or priests. The challenge was on the basis of two related features: the special position that Israel held with respect to the covenant Lord, and a dynamic engagement of the people with the divinely given laws.

While at one time in biblical interpretation the prophets were regarded primarily as 'foretellers' predicting the future—and, from a Christian perspective, the distant future that Christ fulfilled—they then became viewed as 'forth-tellers', applying the norms of God to the situations of their day. We need to allow for an element of both. Clearly they did challenge and cajole Israel back into line as God's people, but the prophets were also concerned with announcing the outworkings of the broken relationship with God for individuals and nations in the future. (The issue of whether a prophet's words came to pass was one key to establishing their validity.) Often this future was a fairly imminent one, no more than days or years away, but as the prophets worked out the implications of God's grace and the permanency of God's promises, they also looked forward to restoration and the application of hope in a more distant future. Here, although it is very rare that the words applied to individuals as opposed to the future of the community of God's people, at the core of this process of restoration the picture of an individual who later became known as 'Messiah' began to take shape.

It is completely misleading to reduce the prophets to moralizing preachers. They were dynamic characters, empowered and directed by the God who shaped the future and revealed it to them. Their speaking of the future was probably seen as a factor in bringing it about, so their responsibility, and eventually their authority, was huge.

NOTES

1 There might be other explanations, including the possibility that he rejects the word used for 'prophet' here because it is a northern title, but accepts as appropriate an alternative word, which we still translate as 'prophet'.

2 J. Lindblom, *Prophecy in Ancient Israel* (Blackwell, 1962), p. 215.

3 'Thus says the Lord' is the most common one. For further details, see C. Westermann, *Basic Forms of Prophetic Speech* (Westminster John Knox, 1991).

Chapter 9

ENGAGING THE CULTURE: EXAMINING WISDOM WITHIN THE BIBLE

'Wisdom' writing can be approached from various angles. For instance, as a 'genre', it encompasses a range of literature from the pithy sayings we associate with Proverbs, through to parables and stories such as those associated with Joseph, or even the succession of David to the throne, and on to the anguished debate on difficult topics that is portrayed *par excellence* within Job. It can be viewed sociologically, linking it to the schools for training young men to become state bureaucrats (in Solomon's era, for example; see also Daniel), or it can be viewed theologically.

PROVERBS

Our point of departure is with some of the sayings in Proverbs, which probably come most readily to our minds when we think of 'Wisdom'. Here are a few illustrations of those short and sometimes enigmatic sayings.

A Without the help of an ox there can be no crop,
   but with a strong ox a big crop is possible. (Proverbs 14:4)

B It isn't clever to get drunk!
   Drinking makes a fool of you and leads to fights. (Proverbs 20:1)

C One wise person can defeat a city full of soldiers and capture their fortress. (Proverbs 21:22)

D An angry king roars like a lion,
   but when a king is pleased, it's like dew on the crops. (Proverbs 19:12)

E The king is a friend to all who are sincere and speak with kindness.
   (Proverbs 22:11)

F Young people take pride in their strength,
   but the grey hairs of wisdom are even more beautiful. (Proverbs 20:29)

G If you plan and work hard, you will have plenty;
   if you get in a hurry, you will end up poor. (Proverbs 21:5)

H Even when the land of the poor produces good crops,
   they get cheated out of what they grow. (Proverbs 13:23)

I A secret bribe will save you from someone's fierce anger. (Proverbs
   21:14)

J Crooks accept secret bribes to keep justice from being done.
   (Proverbs 17:23)

K The Lord hates dishonest scales and dishonest weights.
   So don't cheat! (Proverbs 20:23)

L It's wrong to hate others,
   but God blesses everyone who is kind to the poor. (Proverbs 14:21)

M How can we know what will happen to us
   when the Lord alone decides? (Proverbs 20:24)

N Respect and obey the Lord! This is the beginning of wisdom.
   To have understanding, you must know the Holy God. (Proverbs 9:10)

This small selection gives us a sense of the range of approaches found in
Proverbs, but does not adequately reflect the comprehensiveness of lifestyle issues that are covered. To gain a better perspective, it is worth
reading a few whole chapters, such as chapters 3, 8, 10, 17, and 22—24.
Nevertheless, what can we discern as characteristics from this limited
selection?

Our first proverb, A, appears to be a straightforward agricultural
observation about oxen, ploughing and the resulting crops. Within the

context of the book of Proverbs, though, we must question whether rather more is intended than this. Is the proverb meant primarily as an observation on human behaviour? If so, what is its intention? Does it mean that if you want to succeed you need to find someone strong enough or powerful enough to help you to get the results you want? Or is there some other meaning that is less obvious to us?

Proverb C is another apparently plain observation, but this time it is not focused on the natural world but on military strategy. Obviously it is also affirming the significance of the 'wise' in relationship to the military. Was there a specific historical event that led to the formulation of this proverb, such as the way David captured Jerusalem (2 Samuel 5:6–9)? Or was it fundamentally a piece of propaganda, which could reflect power struggles within the royal court?

· Proverb D is also, at its simplest, an observation of how kings behave, although here it is presented as a comparison: kings roar like lions. This could simply mean that they make a great noise when they are angry, so people should be cautious but shouldn't let the noise worry them too much; or perhaps it implies that when a king roars like a lion there is real danger: he is hungry and angry and likely to attack. The real significance, however, probably lies in the comparison between the first line of the proverb and the second: that kings can make a frightening noise but they can also bring you great prosperity. Presumably the point is that it is worth risking their anger for the benefits that may accrue. Although this proverb appears to be a report of observed facts (both about kings and the natural world and the similarities between them), it is therefore really a motivational saying.

Proverb E is also a statement about kings, but, rather than reflecting arbitrary behaviour and its consequences, this one seems to indicate a seriousness and fairness in their behaviour. Rulers are not capricious; nor, for that matter, are they susceptible to bribes or other kinds of favouritism. They respect those who are sincere and kind and so help to uphold justice. In doing this, they are reflecting the character and nature of God, who also responds positively to those who are sincere and kind, as other proverbs make clear (K and L, for instance). Although this latter point is in no way stated or even hinted at in Proverb E, it is hard not to think that it would resonate in the minds of godly Israelites.

In view of the possibility that the Wisdom tradition flourished during the monarchy and that it was promulgated for young men who were being trained to serve the monarchic establishment, it is tempting to read such comments about kings and rulers as evidence for this royal connection. This is not necessarily the case, however, as there is not a significant proportion of proverbs focusing on kings. Also, as kings were clearly very powerful, it is only to be expected that some attention would be given to how to handle them wisely.

Proverbs B and F–H indicate various levels of observation about human behaviour, from the fairly straightforward and predictable comment about drunkenness (very pertinent if you want to educate people in being wise), to the statement about the value of older people (probably propaganda driven by senior citizens, although it could have been penned by a young scholar wanting to gain approval). It is also noteworthy that proverb F does not minimize the benefits of youth so much as identifying the particular benefit of each age.

Turning to the comments about bribes (I and J), it is fascinating to note how conflicting the two observations are. This is a mark of many popular proverbs, as we say both 'look before you leap' and 'he who hesitates is lost'. The issue to consider here is whether these contrasting views simply cancel one another out. Do they lead to the conclusion that it doesn't matter what you do, which way you respond? I don't think so. Applying wisdom is not a matter of applying the right rules. The rules are only part of the task: they are a resource but are not, in themselves, the whole solution. The two perspectives act initially as a check, leading us to ask: should I review the situation before I decide to act, or is a quick decision the overriding factor? Like a good military leader who has a number of weapons at his disposal, the wise person selects the right approach or guideline to fit the circumstances. To be able to do this, the person needs to discern the exact nature of the circumstances: in other words, they need to be wise.

We need to remember that behind this collection of proverbs is a much deeper level of understanding, which is necessary if someone is going to be truly wise. How is this level of discernment reached? How does an archer hit the target? Both a coach and endless hours of practice are required, as well as knowing how to use the equipment.

Proverbs J and K together indicate different angles on aspects of justice in the community. Some of them—such as the comment on false weights —can be paralleled throughout the ancient Near East, and in Israel's law codes as well as in the seventh- and eighth-century prophets. These kinds of proverbs make it clear that some of the Wisdom material was applicable to many aspects of Israel's life and faith. It is interesting to note that only one of the two we have highlighted—proverb K—brings in God overtly. Nevertheless, we should probably appreciate that people would have understood that God was behind all the other similar sayings too: they were linked to law codes that would have been related to the people's worship experience and to the prophets, who sought to remind people that these requirements were integral to their relationship with God.

It will be obvious that the link between proverbs K–N is the fact that they all do bring God overtly into the frame, but they do it in remarkably varied ways. K uses the reference to God as the motivation for behaving in a just and fair way, but expresses the message in an inverted and very visual way. Proverb L is less direct but equally telling. Presumably, 'others' in the first line means something like 'the poor' in the second; otherwise there appears to be no way of linking the two statements. Here, however, it is God's positive attitude to a group of people that provides the motivation for right behaviour. How exactly this motivation was thought to operate is more open to debate. We could understand the proverb to be saying, 'Be like God and bless the poor', or we could hear a challenge: 'Don't seek to harm the poor, because they are under God's blessing, so if you do them harm you can expect to suffer for it.'

Taken together, these two sayings raise the question of whether, behind every suggestion, direction or command, there is the sense that God is at work—that to do right, to be wise, is to go with the grain of the universe and, conversely, that to invest in evil, or to be foolish, is to strain against God.

Proverb M moves even further in the recognition that all life is influenced and shaped by God, but brings with it a strange twist. As long as we can be sure of the way that God is running the universe, then our choice is in one sense simple: 'Do it God's way—or else!' Once troublesome experiences are allowed to enter the frame, however, this perspective becomes rather disturbing. Rather than encouraging people to behave well because God will support such behaviour and bless such people, it brings to the fore either fatalism ('It won't make any difference what I do, because God is shaping it all anyway') or, even worse, the sort of resignation that parades through the book of Ecclesiastes. This position is also reached if we begin to lose the sense that God behaves according to his revealed will and according to the instructions he has given in the Torah. If we cannot know what God is up to, and if his purposes determine outcomes, what then?

Finally, we can consider proverb N, which addresses a fascinating and fundamental issue. Phrases like this appear many times in the Wisdom material and also in Deuteronomy. At the very least, they underline the fact that being wise is not simply about applying rules. There is the need for a particular attitude towards God as the basis for using wisdom effectively. As poems like Proverbs 8 show, this insight can be presented in even more profound and fluid ways, highlighting the fact that wisdom is woven into the fabric of the universe. It is not arbitrary or superficial, but taps into deep levels of life, and ultimately into the very nature of God himself.

Unfortunately, it would take too long to explore here what this fascinating and elusive proverb could tell us about how wisdom can be acquired and how relating to God in this way meshes with other understandings.[1] Already, however, we can begin to sense something of the richness that lies within even apparently straightforward observations of the everyday world and the human life within it.

It is important to note that the longer, epic treatments of difficult issues (particularly the books of Job and Ecclesiastes) are also full of these pithy sayings. For example, at one point Job says, 'If you want to learn, then go and ask the wild animals and the birds, the flowers and the fish. Any of them can tell you what the Lord has done' (Job 12:7–9). It is equally worthy of note that big issues can be raised in a much more succinct way than in the book of Job, as in Psalm 73, which addresses the suffering of the righteous.

We should also recognize that, within Proverbs, there are some longer and more in-depth reflections, most notably in chapter 8 with its amazing eulogy (mostly in the first person singular) on the subject of wisdom. Right at the heart of this book, which could easily be regarded as no more than an anthology of wise sayings, is the recognition that despite its great range, from platitudes based on rather superficial observations to profound theological statements, there is some way in which all these elements cohere, sharing a fundamental source. What is this source and how can it be discovered and used properly?

RECOVERING WISDOM

Over the last century and more, this rich vein of biblical material has tended to have its significance downplayed. There are a number of reasons for this, including the fact that under the driving engine of the Enlightenment 'received wisdom', or tradition, was not greatly valued. Also, several tendencies within scholarly research have had the effect of marginalizing the importance of Wisdom for Israel's faith. Among these are the views that the idea of God as creator (portrayed in Genesis 1—2) was a late and therefore secondary element in Israel's beliefs, with theological priority being given to the historical basis of her faith, relating her identity to the exodus events.

Viewed from within the biblical traditions, however, it is proper to see 'Wisdom' as one of the core ways in which Israel recognized her links with and relationship to surrounding cultures and attempted to explore the implications of this recognition. This can be illustrated by looking at a couple of expert opinions.

According to Robert Gordis, 'The discovery and elucidation of ancient oriental literature has made it clear that Hebrew Wisdom was not an isolated creation in Israel. On the contrary it was part of a vast intellectual tradition that had been cultivated for centuries throughout the lands of the Fertile Crescent.'[2]

This view is endorsed by Gerhard von Rad, who stated:

To a greater extent than is the case in any other intellectual or religious sphere, Israel's wisdom has borrowed from neighbouring cultures. Indeed she perhaps first learned through her familiarity with foreign wisdom to see correctly the real importance of many of the basic human questions. But what she borrowed she incorporated into the sphere of a belief in God and an understanding of reality which were different from those of her neighbours.[3]

The significant point here is not simply that a connection can be established by comparing Israel's Wisdom sayings with those of Egypt, but that this connection between Israel and the wider world is part of Israel's consciousness and she views it positively: it enhances rather than detracts from the value of her Wisdom sayings and approaches. We can note, for instance, that neither Job nor his friends are presented as

Israelites, but their complex testimony is firmly grounded within the Old Testament canon.

Consistent with this, there is a tendency to use generic names for God, rather than Yahweh, in the Wisdom materials.[4] This would establish the appeal and relevance of the writings to a wide audience; it may also reflect their roots in creation-based thinking, mentioned below. While this is an important indicator, however, we need to keep a balance in trying to understand the implications. It is unlikely to be chance that led to the use of 'Yahweh' in the prologue and epilogue of Job; nor is it adequate merely to argue that these sections were added later. For a proper theological understanding of the book, it has to be read with these elements as an integral part: they provide the context and so become a way of claiming that what might otherwise be regarded as a sort of general religious investigation is actually wrestling with Israel's God. This contextualization acts like a magnetic force that reshapes everything.

So where, theologically speaking, is the foundation for Wisdom as far as Israel is concerned? Even that snappy comment in Job 12:7–9 points us in the right direction: it is to do with the created world. Proverbs 8 amplifies this:

> From the beginning, I [that is, 'Wisdom'] was with the Lord.
> I was there before he began to create the earth.
> At the very first, the Lord gave life to me...
> My birth was before mountains were formed
> or hills were put in place.
> PROVERBS 8:22–23, 25

The grounding of this reflection, then, is in creation: it runs something like this. One God created all the world and all the peoples of this world. It is his world, so the deep-level structures that underpin a successful individual and family, as well as both communal and international life, are actually 'written into' the world by God. At the same time, they are more or less accessible to anyone who either seeks for them or stumbles across them through the experiences of their life.[5] Essentially, they do not require specific revelation, although there is no reason why God cannot give such truths in this way as well. Indeed, those who know God through special revelation will probably be able to perceive more clearly and more readily the footprints of God in the structures of ordinary life.

This is one meaning of the frequent claim that 'the fear of the Lord is the beginning of wisdom'. Understood along these lines, wisdom becomes a bridge from the special community of Israel, with its covenantal relationship with God, to all other peoples.

In some eras of Israel's history, the hope is expressed that non-Israelite people will recognize the quality of wisdom that Israel projects and so be drawn towards her God (see, for instance, Deuteronomy 4:6 and 1 Kings 10:1–13). It is around 'wisdom', however, that Israel can have conversations with non-Israelites about anything, with the underlying certainty that her God is the source of all true wisdom. In summary, wisdom is intimately related to a creationally based theology and is to do with shared truth rather than special revelation, continuous truth rather than the historically revealed, and what is generally applicable rather than what is cult-, ritual- or religion-specific. It is an 'everyday theology', but one in which Israel, with her eyes of faith, should excel.

It is actually quite difficult to draw firm boundaries between what is and is not 'Wisdom' compared, for instance, with law or prophecy. Much that appears in Wisdom writings covers similar territory to many of Israel's laws (see pp. 66–68), and the prophets make frequent use of Wisdom sayings, rhetoric and motifs. Looking from the other direction, the book of Job incorporates a ritual element or two (Job 4:12–21). Often, Wisdom elements are incorporated into the historical accounts, and even large sections, such as the succession narrative in 2 Samuel and 1 Kings, can be defended as inherently Wisdom-like. Some scholars wish to draw a straight line from Wisdom to apocalyptic, while others link apocalyptic fundamentally to prophecy.

It can be claimed with some level of legitimacy that the overt status of Wisdom as primary revelation is different from other parts of the Old Testament.[6] Even this point has to be qualified, for Wisdom is recognized to be a divine (if not the divine) gift to Solomon and is described as an attribute of the Spirit of the Lord in relation to the ideal king in Isaiah 11:2. Also, one of the wise men in Job claims that his wisdom came by a night-time revelation. Equally, it is difficult to escape the claim that 'the fear of the Lord is the beginning of wisdom' (see, for instance, Job 28:28; Proverbs 1:20; compare Job 32:8; Ecclesiastes 2:26) is making a bid for revelatory status.

There are also hidden, or at least deep-level, links between Wisdom and Torah. As Deuteronomy indicates, keeping God's laws will lead people to recognize that Israel is wise: 'If you faithfully obey them when you enter the land, you will show other nations how wise you are. In fact, everyone who hears about your laws will say, "That great nation certainly is wise"' (Deuteronomy 4:6).

Psalm 1 feels as though it is claiming the whole of Israel's worship as an aspect of Wisdom, while Wisdom motifs, as we have already noted, appear in several other psalms. The ultimate outcome that prophet, Torah and Wisdom offer is that of blessing and a fruitful, prosperous life.

Wisdom is not a hermetically sealed unit. There are many interchanges of form, function, content and personnel between the various strands of biblical material. Canonically they all belong together, which may well imply that for the church to be healthy and serve the purposes of God fully, something similar needs to be manifest in her being and doing too.

NOTES

1 For those who find this too tantalizing, have a look at some or all of these references, noting contexts, implications, parallelism and other clues: Exodus 14:31; Deuteronomy 4:10; 6:2; 10:12; 1 Samuel 12:14; Job 28:28; Psalm 25:12–15; 31:19; 103:13–17; 111:10; 147:11; Proverbs 1:7, 20, 29; 8:13; 15:16, 33; Ecclesiastes 12:13.

2 See 'Wisdom and Job' in *Old Testament Issues*, ed. S. Sandmel (SCM Press, 1969), p. 216.

3 G. von Rad, *Wisdom in Israel* (SCM Press, 1972), p. 317.

4 See the claim of W. Gordis in *Old Testament Issues* p. 231. Caution is required for his claim that YHWH only occurs in Proverbs in 10:1–22 and 16:22–29. In the latter case there don't seem to be any, but there are several in the earlier verses of this chapter and verse 33. More generally, there are many references: see, for example, Proverbs 2:6; 14:26; 15:3, 8, 11, 25.

5 Von Rad speaks of 'the self-revelation of the orders of creation' (*Wisdom in Israel*, p. 317). He amplifies this by claiming that from the very beginning there was 'the unwavering certainty that creation herself will reveal her truths to the man who becomes involved with her and trusts her'.

6 'The *Hokmah* of the biblical sages, unlike the Torah of the priests or the Vision of the prophets, usually made no claim to being divine revelation.' Gordis, *Old Testament Issues*, p. 216.

PART FOUR

BEYOND THE TEXT

Chapter 10

MONOTHEISM, MISSION AND MESSIAH

We have been looking at the Old Testament from various angles and, in the process, have introduced ourselves to a range of methods that can enhance our appreciation of the rich materials we find there. Several times we have used the analogy of visiting a cathedral to help us understand the kind of approach we are taking. For a moment, let us return to that analogy. The cathedral has an architectural story to tell, but the materials used for its construction have a geological story as well. One question the Old Testament poses is how far we can go back into the origins of the materials. We would probably say that the way the actual building materials for the cathedral were formed geologically is of interest only in so far as it helps us understand, say, the durability of the stone and how easily the carvings were shaped in it. The cathedral will also have a historical story to tell, as various parts will have been constructed at different times and relate to a broader cultural and social history. There may well be deeply personal aspects to the cathedral too, as we find out why and when various artefacts were given to it.

Beyond all this, though, we miss the point of the building altogether if we neglect the purpose for which the cathedral was consecrated: namely, to be a place of worship, a building which facilitates and enhances the worship of God the Father, Son and Holy Spirit. This purpose is not neutralized by the fact that it may have been constructed as a status symbol for some great nobleman, or the fact that it may have been used as a prison or even a stable at some point in its history. In the end, the edifice cannot be properly appreciated without reference to its ultimate objective. It is not a museum or an art gallery, or a restaurant or shop (although these functions may be fulfilled within it).

In a similar way, although we have explored the Old Testament from various angles, the stubborn fact remains that it was put together only because people had faith in their God—and it was this same God to whom Jesus attributed his origins and his destiny. To neglect this dimension of the Old Testament is to miss the point. In this final section, therefore, we are going to look at some ways to value the Old Testament from within our Christian tradition.

MONOTHEISM

Over the last couple of centuries, one of the ways the Old Testament has been valued and evaluated is in relation to monotheism. The idea of monotheism was perceived to be a central contribution of the Old Testament to religious development, to the progress towards the 'higher religion'.[1] It was seen to be a distinguishing mark of Jewish/Old Testament faith in contrast with Greek and Roman religions, the seed-beds in which Christianity was born.

For some (reading the Old Testament superficially, perhaps), it seemed that the whole of the Old Testament, as well as all its parts, clearly presupposed and proclaimed that there is only one God and that there could only ever be one God. For 19th-century scholars developing critical vision, however, the story became rather that the Hebrews originally believed in several gods and that, over their faith journey of 1500 years, they proceeded through the stages of animism (the belief that all kinds of objects and natural things such as trees and streams were indwelt by spirits) and polytheism (the belief that there are many gods and goddesses), towards the only rationally defensible view that there is only one supreme deity, one absolute ground of being, the high God.

In parts of the 20th century, the debate was somewhat different. It was concerned with the extent to which 'monotheism' was an appropriate term to apply to Old Testament beliefs about God(s). Various other terms were tried out, such as monolatry (meaning the worship of only one god: a parallel word to idolatry),[2] monarchical theism (the belief that while there may be other gods, one god is supreme among them) and practical monotheism (the view that as far as a particular people was concerned, there was only one god to whom they gave allegiance, although there might in theory be others that affected different groups of people).

Practical monotheism was seeking to deal with three issues at once. Firstly, it did not wish to give up the very strong link between Israel's view of God and the view that was highly valued within the Jewish, Christian and even secular philosophical traditions: namely, that there can only be one supreme deity. Secondly, it faced squarely the fact that Israel's view of God was not formed primarily as the outcome of philosophical reflection or speculation but as a result of her understanding of her historical experiences. Finally, those who supported this perspective wanted to do justice to the Old Testament materials themselves. Practical monotheism can be summarized as the view that only one god is significant for us; we only give allegiance to this one god; and it is this god, this faith stream, this story and this community nourished by that story, which flow into the New Testament and to which Jesus gives his allegiance. Through Jesus it is this understanding (with its faith commitment as a necessary presupposition) that is owned by the Christian church.

There are several advantages to the position of practical monotheism. The most obvious is that the view that there is only one God no longer has to be established as an abstract philosophical or theological claim before it can be considered valid. Secondly, it is not disproved by the apparent acknowledgment (or recognition of the possibility) within parts of the Old Testament of the existence of or influence of other deities within other nations. Thirdly, it emphasizes that Israel's belief structure was a matter of living rather than thinking, of commitments and practice rather than theory, of behaviour more than debate. Finally, it acts as a warning not to try to squeeze Hebrew views into the deistic modes of philosophy, but creates genuine space for the Old Testament's understanding to challenge us, even if there might appear to be toleration towards the possibility that other deities might exist within the passages under consideration.

This very superficial account of the Old Testament and monotheism alerts us to the fact that the concept of 'monotheism' was itself a distorting lens when applied to the Old Testament. It brought with it a whole mass of social and philosophical baggage, and there was a tacit assumption that if Israelite thoughts about God failed to fit this approach, then that itself was good grounds for rejecting it all.

How will we know, though, whether two people who claim to worship one god are really worshipping the same reality? Is it enough that they use the same name for their god? What if they use different names but base their worship on the same events? Can they worship at different shrines and still be worshipping the same god? What if their rituals are different or incompatible, or they make conflicting claims about this god? What if they kill one another in the name of this god? And what happens if two groups or individuals start off by thinking that their gods are different (or if each one thinks its own god is real and the other's is not), then get together, conflate their views, rituals and behaviours and affirm that they do worship the same god? Does that make it so?

None of these issues is simple, and the many possibilities make it quite difficult to know how we can establish that Israel worshipped only one God, let alone that this amounts to monotheism. What is worth doing, however, is to look at a few key texts, which seem to indicate that Israel recognized the absolute priority of one God for them, and which have gone on to be influential in the Christian tradition too.

- Genesis 1 (God as creator of all and with commitment to all)
- Exodus 20 (the Ten Commandments: 'worship no God but me')
- Deuteronomy 6:4 (The Lord is one)
- Amos 9:5–7 (God's concern for and control over all nations)
- Isaiah 40 (God's uniqueness and incomparability)
- Psalms 93—97 (God's universal kingship)

One way to appreciate the contribution of such texts is to imagine our Christian faith without them. Take these elements away from our understanding of God, and I doubt whether many of us would recognize such a deity as the one we are committed to worship and to whom we dedicate our lives.

Perhaps, of all these texts, Deuteronomy 6:4 has been the most influential. Its recognition and resonance can be traced in many places in both Old and New Testaments, as well as being fundamental for the Jewish faith and implicitly for Christianity and Islam. 'Israel, remember this! The Lord—and the Lord alone—is our God. Love the Lord your God with all your heart, with all your soul, and with all your strength. Never forget these commandments that I am giving you today. Teach them to your children' (Deuteronomy 6:4–7a, GNB).

We can only make a few superficial comments about this amazing text.

- The appeal to 'remember' recalls Israel's history with God.
- There is a very exclusive claim, that only Yahweh is Israel's God.
- This claim is exclusive but not absolute: it does not say that there is no other god in existence, or that it is inappropriate for other peoples to relate to other gods. It does not explicitly claim that Yahweh only relates to this people and not to other peoples, but equally it does not

make the claim, or even implicitly suggest, that Yahweh does relate or even wants to relate to other peoples in the same way, either. It is rather more open in its implications than might at first appear.

- The proper recognition of this specific and exclusive relationship is not only or primarily intellectual. It is not, as it tended to become in the development of the Enlightenment concept of monotheism, a self-evident truth of reason that people are obliged to accept. The appropriate response is love: that is, an absolute and exclusive positive relationship that involves commitment of the whole person—heart, soul, strength.
- It is nevertheless a reality that can be communicated to others: 'teach [these commandments] to your children'. There is no imperative to communicate them to all peoples, but only to those who are involved in this community and its relationship to this one God.

There are two more themes that are closely linked to the kinds of views about God that we have been considering, which are also significant within the Christian tradition. This does not mean that, in some way, they are logical deductions or necessary outcomes, but rather that they make good sense when understood in relationship to one another. The two themes are the mission of God, and the coming of Messiah.

THE MISSION OF GOD [3]

In the light of our final comment about Deuteronomy 6:4–6 (that there is no imperative to communicate God's commands to all people), it may seem strange to claim that mission relates to monotheism. If this key text for Jewish and Christian belief in one God does not lead on to the practice of mission, what can be the connection? The drive towards a universal mission imperative arises from the following points taken together.

- The biblical account helps us to understand who God is and therefore what our response to and responsibility for this God should be.
- The account begins by presenting this God as responsible for creating the whole universe, especially the whole earth and all its peoples.
- It also indicates that this God values and is concerned for all peoples.
- This God works from particulars to universals: he calls Abraham, but

his purpose is to bless all peoples (Genesis 12:1–3). He calls and commits himself to Israel, but his horizon always encompasses the total community of peoples.

- This God expresses his commitment by involvement in passionate relationship, by effective action to benefit his people and by his commitment to seek to shape this people to be like him.
- As his embrace includes all peoples, there is an insistent pressure both from within his people and from without, through the call of God to them, to move towards others with the story of God that includes them.
- The rationale for this all-inclusive relationship has to be that this God is either the only god there is, or at least the god who is best for all peoples, or who has the strongest claim on the allegiance of all peoples.

From time to time, and in many different ways, this 'mission imperative' breaks out of the text. We have already noted, for instance, the call of Abraham in Genesis 12:1–3, where God promises to bless all nations through him. It is strikingly present too in some of the psalms, where the universal kingship of God is celebrated. Here is one example.

> *Sing a new song to the Lord!*
> *Sing to the Lord, all the world!*
> *Sing to the Lord, and praise him!*
> *Proclaim every day the good news that he has saved us.*
> *Proclaim his glory to the nations,*
> *his mighty deeds to all peoples.*
> PSALM 96:1–3 (GNB)

With these psalms, there is a strong connection between the superiority of Israel's God and his role in creation: 'The gods of all other nations are only idols, but the Lord created the heavens' (Psalm 96:5, GNB).

It might be possible to interpret Psalm 96:1–3 to indicate that Israel is domineering over other nations: proclaiming God's glory to the other nations could be the equivalent of pointing out to them that God has saved Israel at their expense. Verses 7–8 suggest otherwise, however, as they invite all peoples not only to 'praise his glory and might' but also to come into God's temple. Here, the sanctuary itself and, with it (we must presume), access to Israel's God are opened up to the whole world. It is

Israel's task and privilege to announce what God has done, as well as his supremacy over other gods, to the nations, as a prelude to inviting them to join Israel at the heart of her worship.

There are several highlights in the later part of Isaiah. After the verses telling us that Cyrus, a foreign ruler, has been chosen by Yahweh to help Israel, by releasing them from exile in Babylon, God continues, 'I do this so that everyone from one end of the world to the other may know that I am the Lord and that there is no other god' (Isaiah 45:6, GNB). Later in the same chapter we read, 'Turn to me now and be saved, people all over the world! I am the only God there is' (v. 22, GNB).

It is important to underline the fact that this is not only God's position, but also the mission he gives to his 'servant', although whether this person is understood as the nation or an individual is difficult to determine: 'The Lord said to me, "I have a greater task for you, my servant. Not only will you restore to greatness the people of Israel who have survived, but I will also make you a light to the nations—so that all the world may be saved"' (Isaiah 49:6, GNB).

Later, the prophet also has this to say about the 'servant' who has suffered complete humiliation and rejection: 'But now many nations will marvel at him, and kings will be speechless with amazement. They will see and understand something they had never known' (52:15, GNB).

Throughout these chapters, there is a strong insistence on the uniqueness and superiority of Yahweh with respect to the other 'gods', linked with the theme of God's role as creator. The reference to 'understanding' and also 'light' may well indicate that not far away are the influences of the Wisdom tradition in Israel's faith.

The theme of the inclusion of the nations can also be found in the early chapters of Isaiah, especially 2:1–5. The theme emerges in other places too, and in many different ways. The story of Ruth contains it on a personal level, while the prophet Jonah provides a larger canvas with his unwanted success in Nineveh, where his reluctantly delivered message prompts wholesale repentance.

Zechariah 14 is in many ways a strange chapter, telling a complex story of God's judgment on both Jerusalem and the nations, with terrible pictures of death by earthquake, plague and military action. We then reach a tranquil place, however: 'Then all the survivors from the nations that have attacked Jerusalem will go there each year to worship the Lord Almighty as king, and to celebrate the Festival of Shelters' (Zechariah

14:16, GNB). (For an exploration of the Festival of Shelters, see pages 52–56.)

Of course, it cannot be argued that everyone in Israel felt this way about their faith, or that a majority of the biblical witness contains this presupposition, or even that there is a chronological progression from exclusivism to universalism. There is evidence, though, that from time to time the pressure of God's purpose breaks through the concerns of the times or the limitations of the writers, so that we glimpse the big plan of God to offer himself to all peoples. But it could also be argued that such a reading neglects the majority of the texts and the overall direction of the majority of the Old Testament's message. How, then, can we justify privileging the bigger vision that God wishes his blessing to reach all peoples and for them to respond positively to him? This question is one that we will pick up in the next chapter.

THE MESSIAH OF GOD

In various places and with varied images, the Old Testament looks towards future events. Normally, it seems that these events were expected to come to pass within a generation or two, but at the same time they represent what we might describe as an 'enriched future'. It is this better quality of life that is significant, rather than how near or far from coming to pass the specific future events were imagined to be.

Often this 'enriched future' is pictured in rather idealized human terms of prosperity, peace and security: 'Everyone will live in peace among his own vineyards and fig trees, and no one will make him afraid. The Lord Almighty has promised this' (Micah 4:4, GNB; compare Jeremiah 31:12). On other occasions it is the uniting of the divided nation that takes centre stage, as in Ezekiel 37:15–28, where God tells Ezekiel to join together two sticks to symbolize this unity.

For Jeremiah, it is a new covenant that provides the focal point, although, interestingly, the reference to 'a new covenant with the people of Israel and with the people of Judah' (31:31, GNB) may carry the same message as Ezekiel, of unifying the divided nation.

Often, the picture includes Israel's victory over or deliverance from her enemies, whatever the particular circumstances may suggest. In the memorable words of Isaiah 40:1, 10: '"Comfort my people," says our

God. "Comfort them!" ... The Sovereign Lord is coming to rule with power, bringing with him the people he has rescued' (GNB).

Many scholars have had great fun trying to synthesize a cohesive picture of this promised future from all the clues in the texts, as well as seeking to identify the sources for the images and depictions of this hope. Both are difficult challenges.

One particular feature that can be noted is that the hope frequently involves a human person who brings it about. Again, this person has many different characteristics and functions. In Deuteronomy we find mention of a prophet like Moses: 'Instead, he will send you a prophet like me from among your own people, and you are to obey him' (Deuteronomy 18:15, GNB; compare verse 18). Often the person is thought of as a king or military ruler:

A child is born to us! A son is given to us! And he will be our ruler. He will be called, 'Wonderful Counsellor', 'Mighty God', 'Eternal Father', 'Prince of Peace'. His royal power will continue to grow; his kingdom will always be at peace. He will rule as King David's successor, basing his power on right and justice, from now until the end of time.
ISAIAH 9:6–7 (GNB)

Jeremiah and Ezekiel have their own versions of this theme, as we can see in Jeremiah 33:14–26 and Ezekiel 37:24–27. It is interesting that within both of these passages there is reference to 'my servant David' (Jeremiah 33:22, 26; Ezekiel 37:24–25), although in Jeremiah he is the reason why God will restore Israel, and in Ezekiel he provides the model. In both cases, though, the king-figure is central to God's promise.

In Jeremiah 33, there is also the promise of prosperity for the levitical priests and the recognition that God has a covenant with them, which also drives his commitment to restore the nation. In Zechariah 4 there is a vision of two olive trees, which again probably represents the combination of royal and priestly leadership.

As we read the prophets, we can see that they show the tension of holding together a variety of truths that seem in perpetual conflict within Israel's actual historical experience. These truths include the fact that God has made binding promises to Israel—or at least to its king, to Jerusalem and to its temple—that he must punish the waywardness and rebellion of his people, or cease to be both holy and all-powerful. Such punishment, expressed as it was through exile, in fact brings disgrace on God as well as his people, and this becomes an intolerable position to maintain. For this reason, but also because he is faithful to his commitments and loving to his people, God must act to rectify the disrupted situations.

The resolution that begins to emerge, although it is rarely if ever fully formed, is that God will act through a person, his servant, whom he will appoint and send. This action will not be a straightforward military intervention, because that would not sort out the aspects of the situation concerned with morality and the relationship with God. As a result, the process takes on more sombre tones, indicating suffering on behalf of others in order to bring release not only from captivity but also from the slavery of disobedience and deception.

So, in Zechariah 4:6–7 we have the message to King Zerubbabel, who is represented as one of the olive trees: 'You will succeed, not by military might or by your own strength, but by my spirit. Obstacles as great as mountains will disappear before you. You will rebuild the Temple, and as you put the last stone in place, the people will shout, "Beautiful, beautiful!"' (GNB).

Meanwhile, in Isaiah 53:10–12 we read:

The Lord says, 'It was my will that he should suffer; his death was a sacrifice to bring forgiveness... After a life of suffering, he will again have joy; he will know that he did not suffer in vain. My devoted servant, with whom I am pleased... And so I will give him a place of honour, a place among the great and powerful. (GNB)

Rarely is this suffering figure linked to the ruler of the line of King David. Although many of the kings did suffer with their people, the usual perspective (as presented in the books of Kings) is that the people are dragged into suffering because of the disobedience of the king, rather than the king suffering because of the people. It seems likely that the 'servants' who are depicted as suffering to redeem the nation are the prophets; after all, as we have seen, they were known as 'my servants the prophets'. H. Wheeler Robinson's book *The Cross in the Old Testament* (SCM, part published in 1916, but published in full in 1955) makes the case very convincingly for Jeremiah as the 'suffering servant' figure in Isaiah 40—55, but we can also include here Hosea with his experience of broken marriage,

Isaiah with some of his sufferings, Ezekiel with his many expressions of deprivation, and so on. It is as though God draws the prophets into his own turmoil as part of the process of redemption, buying back his people and transforming them. The prophets probably did not see themselves in this redemptive role, and naturally, no prophet could present himself thus, but those who collected their writings may well have done so.

What emerges is a sense of the overall purpose of God to invite all nations into relationship with him. In order to pursue this purpose, God calls Israel, but Israel herself slips into disobedience. God uses individuals to call her back to himself, as well as the laws and rituals overseen by the priests. The military rulers play their part by protecting Israel from oppression but they cannot save her from her own disobedience and are often its major source. Somewhere, hidden in Israel's national consciousness, is this bigger purpose of God from which, like gravity, she can never quite escape. It pulls her back to his own purpose, but she cannot fulfil it either. Accordingly, what develops, in fragmentary forms, is the vision of a future person, part priest, part king, part prophet (all of whom, in different ways, represented God to the people and the people to God) who will help Israel to fulfil her God-given mission. This person, whom no one in Israel saw in his entirety, is the person with whom Jesus comes to be identified, the one we so easily refer to as 'Messiah'.[4]

NOTES

1 See the very interesting paper by R. Bauckham, 'Biblical Theology and the Problem of Monotheism' published in *Scripture and Hermeneutics Vol. 5: 'Out of Egypt'* (Paternoster/Zondervan, 2004), pp. 187ff. ('Old Testament scholars have often attached to their accounts of the development of monotheism in ancient Israel remarks to the effect that monotheism was the great Jewish contribution to the world...', p. 203).

2 See, for example, H.H. Rowley, *Faith of Israel* (SCM Press, 1956), p. 72.

3 See, among other books, H.H. Rowley, *The Missionary Message of the Old Testament* (Carey Kingsgate Press, 1944); R. Martin-Achard, *A Light to the Nations* (Olive and Boyd, 1962); J. Blauw, *Missionary Nature of the Church* (Lutterworth, 1962); D. Burnett, *The Healing of the Nations: The Biblical Basis of the Mission of God* (Paternoster, 1980); C. Wright, 'Mission as Matrix for Hermeneutics and Biblical Theology' in *Scripture and Hermeneutics Vol. 5*, pp. 104ff.

4 See C. Wright, 'Mission as Matrix for Hermeneutics and Biblical Theology' in *Scripture and Hermeneutics Vol. 5*, p. 108: 'The Messiah was the promised one who would embody

in his own person the identity and mission of Israel, as their representative, king, leader and saviour. Through the Messiah as his anointed agent, Yahweh the God of Israel would bring about all that he intended for Israel. But what was the mission of Israel? It was nothing less than to be a 'Light to the nations', the means of bringing the redemptive blessing of God to all the nations of the world, as originally promised in the title deeds of the covenant with Abraham... Through the Messiah, therefore, the God of Israel would also bring about all that he intended for the nations.'

Chapter 11

OLD AND NEW: A LEGITIMATE CONNECTION?

To construct the picture of God's mission, as well as to depict the character and role of the Messiah, we have selected aspects of the overall messages, metaphors and proposals of the Old Testament. We have done this partly to follow through the inner logic of the Old Testament itself, but also because we read the Old Testament from the perspectives provided by the New Testament. In other words, our New Testament commitment, driven by our position within the Christian community, means that we prioritize some texts, and some readings of texts, over others. We need to recognize that a Jew or Muslim reading the Old Testament might well prioritize other texts and provide other reconstructions. Is this a problem for us and, if so, what kind of problem?

Consider these very familiar words: 'Jesus then explained everything written about himself in the Scriptures, beginning with the Law of Moses and the Books of the Prophets' (Luke 24:27). This is Luke's very brief summary of what Jesus was doing in that fairly lengthy conversation, as he and two other people journeyed to Emmaus. We all know that the people to whom Jesus was speaking were disciples who had fled Jerusalem with broken hearts and hopes, after the crucifixion of Jesus. This Jesus they described as the one whom they had expected to 'set Israel free' (24:21)—the Messiah.

The two themselves describe what Jesus did as he travelled with them, even more succinctly and more comprehensively than in verse 27: 'He... explained the Scriptures to us' (v. 32).

We should remember that 'the Scriptures' means something like our Old Testament—certainly not the New Testament. We also need to recognize who Luke's audience is. It is not primarily the disciples gathered fearfully together at nightfall on the first Easter Day—although, dramatically, within the story, that is whom we focus on, for the meeting with them is the climax of the frantic journey of Cleopas and his companion as they rush back to Jerusalem. The real audience of Luke's narrative is 'Honourable Theophilus' (Luke 1:3), who is almost certainly a high-ranking Roman. Luke is telling him that the Old Testament, as Jesus read it, was about Jesus himself. When Theophilus reaches Volume Two, the Acts of the Apostles, and turns to Luke's summaries of the apostolic preaching, he can see how the disciples unpacked the Old Testament and related it to Jesus, thus expanding the brief and enticing references in this resurrection story of the Emmaus road (see the preaching of Peter, Stephen, Philip and Paul in Acts 2:14–36; 7:2–53; 8:26–35; 13:15–48). Luke's message is that Jesus, and authentic Christians, relate the Old Testament to Jesus, and not only to Jesus' life and death but also to people's responses to this complex of events as well.

Luke is able to condense dramatically the Emmaus story that the two tell to the Jerusalem disciples (24:35) because he has already given us the account as it happened. This is not his only technique for important messages. Sometimes he underlines the significance of a message or experience by repeating it in different contexts, although the repetitions are never duplicate copies (see, for example, the encounter between Peter and Cornelius: Acts 10; 11:4–17; 15:7–9; and Paul's conversion: Acts 9:1–19; 22:1–16; 26:9–17). In fact, within the Emmaus story, we have already mentally received the message about Jesus expounding the scriptures and relating them to himself and his suffering at least three times (see vv. 27, 32, 35; there is probably a fourth instance, in that once we know the story we also read it back into verse 26).

Luke, in his Gospel, has not yet finished in his work to embed in Gentile minds the importance of the Old Testament and the significance of Jesus and his suffering for a proper understanding of it. In fact, he saves his most expansive treatment of the theme for an even more dramatic moment, when Jesus is appearing to the disciples and establishing his reality to them, before his return to heaven: 'Jesus said to them, "While I was still with you, I told you that everything written about me in the Law of Moses, the Books of the Prophets, and the Psalms had to happen." Then he helped them understand the Scriptures' (Luke 24:44–45).

Now the Psalms are included, and this emphatic endorsement of the Christian reading of scripture is given to all the disciples. Now, for the first time, we hear what Jesus himself has to say about this interpretation. 'He told them: The Scriptures say that the Messiah must suffer, then three days later he will rise from death. They also say that all people of every nation must be told in my name to turn to God, in order to be forgiven' (24:46–47).

The scriptures not only validate what happened to Jesus but also the whole Gentile mission. Theophilus, in hearing the story of Jesus from Luke, is also part of the Old Testament's message. He cannot dismiss it as unnecessary for the Christian faith (as Gentiles have frequently tended to do), because to do so is to spiritually disinherit oneself. The scriptures not only endorse the Messiah but the mission of the one God. According to Luke (and he claims that it has the authority of Jesus), the right way to read the Old Testament is in terms of Jesus and the Christian mission. Much of Acts can be understood as a 'sermonic event': the telling of the story that establishes the meaning of the Old Testament command to tell all peoples of all nations.

There is one other theme that, as Luke tells us, comes as part of the package about the Christian reading of the Old Testament—namely that it isn't obvious or easy to understand the Old Testament this way, unless you are Jesus or see things through his eyes. His first words to the bereaved and traumatized pair of Emmaus disciples are, 'Why can't you understand? How can you be so slow to believe…?' (24:23). When Jesus addresses the eleven disciples at Jerusalem, he claims that he was proclaiming the same message all the time he was with them as rabbi. We also find an emphasis on Jesus clearing away the difficulties. Such phrases as 'Jesus then explained', 'he explained the Scriptures to us' and 'he helped them understand the Scriptures' make this point well. The same problem of understanding and the same necessity for an interpreter comes through many times in Acts. What is being presented for us is that:

- To make sense of the Messiah and the Christian mission, we need to understand the Old Testament properly.
- To understand the Old Testament properly is to see how, in all its major components, it bears witness to Jesus. Suffering is key, though, not oppression or destruction or violence against enemies.
- To understand the Old Testament this way is not easy, however, and only happens within the Christian community as the Holy Spirit enables Christian disciples to understand.
- The Old Testament is not an optional extra, not even for Gentiles (even though keeping most of the laws is not required for them); it is an essential faith document.

We have only explored here one small part of what the New Testament has to say about the significance of the Old Testament, but even this one part should challenge us to recognize that we cannot live a full faith if we turn our backs on, or even neglect, the Old Testament.

Nevertheless, the recognition that other people will read the Old Testament in other ways is implicit in this examination of what Luke is saying. All the accounts of the struggles, both intellectual and physical, that the early Christian community had with the Jews both in Jerusalem and the Diaspora, make this unmistakably clear. Equally clearly, while recognizing that there is a spiritual dimension to the struggle, we find every encouragement to propagate and defend a Christian reading of the Old Testament.

As we take account of the multiplicity of ways in which the Old Testament is used within the New Testament, we can also be encouraged to explore the Old Testament with all the methods at our disposal today. We must also find ways to discern what is of ongoing significance through the filter that Jesus provides, even as we recognize that, to see Jesus properly, we must approach him through the lens of the Old Testament. There should be a dialectic (two-way traffic) from the Old Testament to the New Testament and back again, as well as between the Old Testament and our Christian understanding.

A PROBLEM?

Let us return to the question posed at the beginning of this chapter, whether the possibility of different (that is, non-Christian) readings of the Old Testament is a problem and, if so, what kind of problem.

It is, in fact, no more a problem to us than it was for Jesus or the early Church. There always was a debate about the proper way to read the Old Testament materials; it was one of the grounds of contention between the Christians and Jews, as well as other religious groups that they encountered. We should also remember that there was much variety of interpretation within the various components of Judaism at that time.

Indeed, if there were no problem (that is, no difference in the way Christians read, understand and handle the Old Testament, compared with people who have a different stance), that in itself would be problematic. The Old Testament is not a neutral text; it is a document that only makes sense within a faith community. To understand it properly is a difficult task, which can, from the perspective of the Christian faith, be best accomplished only from within the Christian community. 'Best' means here something like 'in terms of its most significant message'; it certainly does not deny to other scholars from other perspectives the right to investigate the texts within it from different perspectives.

We should not regard as a fatal problem, though, the fact that there is continuing debate among scholars, as well as personal struggle for Christians, about how to value the Old Testament. The challenge to 'understand' is as perennial as the refusal to abandon these ancient texts as part of our scriptures. It does not mean that we should reject all the insights of scholarship, any more than Jesus or the disciples rejected the understanding of Hebrew (which was not their first language), based as it was on the scholarship of their day. It is when scholarship starts to claim that relating the Old Testament to Jesus is improper or unscientific that we must be prepared to take our stand. For us, the Old Testament is not a 'stand-alone' product. It is part of our whole Bible, and to ignore this fact is to forsake our appropriate interpretative context.

How, then, have Christian scholars provided us with insights about how to understand the Old Testament from a Christian perspective? What clues can we appropriate towards creating a 'big picture'?

A CHRISTIAN PERSPECTIVE

At the simplest but perhaps also most profound level is the claim that the God of the Old Testament is the 'Abba' of Jesus, or, as Paul might have put it, 'the God and Father of our Lord Jesus Christ' (Romans 15:6; Ephesians 1:3). Without this bracketing of Jesus' God and the God of the Old Testament, we probably would not be including the Old Testament in our foundational document of faith. This statement sets up a problem, however, rather than providing a solution. As one scholar puts it:

The Christ event does not put this God of the Old Testament in question; it is proclaimed as his own, true, final work. As the final, eschatological act of God, it of course puts all the other works of the same God in the shade. In the light of the revelation of Christ we can also ask whether all the actions and properties attributed to God in the Old Testament really were divine actions and divine properties.[1]

So in what ways can we understand the relationship of the Old Testament to the New Testament? Here, in brief outline, are some responses to this intriguing question.

Law and Gospel

This way of distinguishing the Old Testament from the New Testament is usually traced back to Martin Luther. It has become very influential in the background thinking of Protestant Christians, especially those who relate to an evangelical ethos. Essentially, it proposes that the Old Testament is law—that is, God's righteous demand on people—which brings them to a place of despair before God because, when they pay attention to the law, they find that they cannot fulfil it. Also highlighted is the fact that until they paid attention to the law, they were rebellious anyway. Even if they could now fulfil the law, they would still fall under God's righteous judgment for their previous years of rebellion. The New Testament, by contrast, is God's gracious response to this human predicament, providing us with his solution to our problem of rebellion, disobedience and sinfulness through the cross of Christ.

There are all kinds of weaknesses with this position, including the fact that the Old Testament is by no means all law and the New is by no means all grace, however law and grace are described. Within the Old Testament, there is God's provision for human sinfulness through the sacrificial system, for instance; within the New, there are divine demands as well. Even more fundamentally, we should question whether the function attributed to law within the Old Testament is actually appropriate: remember how we located the laws within the framework of covenant, which is, in fact, a framework of grace (see pp. 58–60, 65).

Antitype and type[2]

This view suggests that events and arrangements within the Old Testament are models or examples (in the sense of being 'less significant', not 'fully functioning') of New Testament events and arrangements. As such, they point forward to the better way that the New Testament provides. The sacrificial system, for example, is an antitype of the sacrifice of Jesus, God's provision for human sinfulness. To be more specific, Abraham's willingness to sacrifice Isaac (the one through whom, according to God himself, the promise of universal blessing was to come) prefigures the willingness of God not to spare his own Son but to give him up for us all.

For many years this proposal was quite out of favour with scholars, as it seemed too arbitrary, at the mercy of the interpreter, as well as rather Platonic in its perceptions (giving a kind of eternal significance to events, as though they were pure ideas and not grounded in specific historical contexts). Over recent decades, however, it has become more popular, partly because it was perceived that the New Testament did use the Old quite often in this kind of way, but also because the approach was aligned with an emphasis on God's acts: the attempt was made to distinguish typology from allegory, on the grounds that the correspondence between Old and New was rooted in history within both Testaments.

It has also been argued that postmodern ways of reading texts make the 'antitype and type' approach more acceptable. It had been criticized, for instance, because typology seemed to read meanings into Old Testament passages that could not have been the intention of the author. The author of the Abraham story could not have had the sacrifice of Jesus in mind, so was it not a mistake to read the New Testament message into the Old? If the supremacy of 'authorial intention' is denied, however, this criticism loses at least some of its bite, for readers are given the right to understand the text in the way that makes fullest sense to them. For an interesting recent reapplication of the Abel story along these lines, see *Truth Is Stranger Than It Used To Be*.[3] This issue of 'authorial intention' can also be utilized in a different way. The Christian view is that God is the ultimate author of scripture, so we cannot assume that it was not in his mind that Christ would die for the sins of the world when he allowed the Abraham–Isaac story to take place, to be written down as part of Genesis and then to be incorporated into the Old Testament as scripture. Such a view does not need to deny that the original human author was limited in his perspective, but it can maintain God's prerogative to convey his own deeper, additional meaning as well.

A number of critical points can be raised about the 'antitype and type' approach. What if other religions see other events and arrangements in the Old Testament (or even interpretations of the same ones) as antitypes to their own religion? What defence against this can be made for the claims of the Christian view? One defence could be that they are rooted in history or in the story of that history. But if we are not seeking to defend the historicity of the events, can we readily distinguish typology from allegory? Also, this approach would seem to cover only a relatively small part of the Old Testament rather than the whole.

Prophecy and fulfilment

We have already considered the Old Testament understanding of prophecy and how predictive it might be. Clearly, the New Testament often uses the Old Testament along these lines, or so it appears. Some of the same arguments for and against the use of the 'antitype and type' approach can apply to 'prophecy and fulfilment' as well. Much Old Testa-ment prophecy, even when it is future-oriented, actually finds fulfilment within the Old Testament itself (for example, the Assyrian destruction of Samaria and the sparing of Jerusalem: see Isaiah 28:1—4; and 37), while the New Testament in many places becomes predictive of the future. Where, then, is the fundamental difference which allows us to say that the Old Testament means prophecy while the New Testament equals fulfilment?

Seeing the equation this way is, therefore, probably inappropriate. Rather than seeing it as a means of distinguishing the Old Testament from the New, we should see it as a uniting tendency. Both Testaments bear witness to the God who operates under the tension of prophecy and its fulfilment, which somehow still leaves the prophecy to be completely fulfilled. The challenge for this approach, then, becomes how we can maintain that the 'Christ event' (meaning all that Jesus, said and did, especially his death, resurrection and ascension, perhaps also incorporating his return in glory) is of a different order of fulfilment from the events that occur within the Old Testament itself.

Furthermore, if the fulfilment of a prophecy does not mean that it becomes redundant, what about all the Old Testament prophecies that we may have disregarded because they have been fulfilled, such as the destruction of Samaria by Assyria? Does that prophecy still have implications, either for the time of the New Testament or now, in that some aspect of it still remains to be fulfilled? Once we step beyond the pages of the New Testament, how do we know what is a valid or an invalid application? The history of the interpretation of the 'Beast' in the book of Revelation provides us with an example of the pitfalls involved.

Promise and fulfilment

A refinement of some of these issues led some 20th-century Old Testament scholars, particularly the German scholars Claus Westermann and Walther Zimmerli, to focus not on specific and very varied, even conflicting, prophecies that required tightly defined events to qualify as their legitimate fulfilment, but rather on what they regarded as a fundamental and pervasive type of commitment that God has given—the promise of God, which not only allowed for, but actually required, repeated fulfilments. As a parallel, if in our marriage vows we promise that we will cherish and be faithful to our partner, there are many events that could qualify as fulfilling this promise, but equally some that would contradict it. No one would expect, if we proved we cherished our partner once, that the commitment in the promise was now over. So it is with God.

What is the fundamental promise that God has given? Can it be defined and restricted any more than specific prophetic predictions? Is it somehow that God will be 'with' people, either as individuals or as a nation? If so, then perhaps we can also claim, from a Christian perspective, a difference of quality in the fulfilment in Christ, for the fundamental claim is that 'God was in Christ', that Jesus is Immanuel (see Isaiah 7:14; Matthew 1:23; John 1:14; 2 Corinthians 5:19). This does not enforce the Christian view of the Old Testament in a literal way, but at least it provides some kind of coherence for the Christian position.

Two questions remain unanswered. Can this kind of promise be established as fundamental for the Old Testament? If so, to what extent does this distinguish the Christian faith from other faiths?

With respect to the first, we can reflect on the idea of 'incarnation'. This idea can be viewed as emerging from, or present embryonically in, the Old Testament. As we all know, the existence of an embryo does not guarantee the development of mature life, but certainly the absence of an embryo makes such life impossible. It is therefore significant that God is present for his people in priestly decisions, that the king was acknowledged as having God's authority, and that some of the prophets are called to experience God's deep suffering for and with his people, in addition to the fact that God's promise to go with, or be with, his people is fundamental for parts of the Old Testament.

With respect to the second question, all we can say here is that it has led to a fascinating scholarly debate.

The focus on the 'promise of God' theme began as an attempt to distinguish between, as well as link, the two Testaments. With all such attempts, one by-product is that we are likely to read the New Testament in an enriched and more lively way. Parts that we may have read rather quickly or superficially can gain a deeper and more comprehensible significance.

History

There have been other attempts, exploring or seeking to exploit the sense that the Old Testament is about God acting in history while the New is about God acting in Christ (and therefore also acting in history). Fundamentally, these attempts start from a wish to establish the linkage between the Testaments, perhaps under the pressure of the history or sociology of religions.

The historical approach is probably the most basic way to view the connection between the two Testaments, and is explained along these lines: Jesus was a Jew, and the Old Testament is the collection of documents that formed the basis of Judaism. It also served to draw together the various strands of Judaism, including the many different understandings of their faith that developed among the Diaspora (the Jews who lived all over the known world, in Egypt as well as those parts dominated by either Greek or Latin cultures). The immediate and obvious problem with this explanation is that the foundational religious texts for such Jews—and even Jesus—was not perhaps the Old Testament precisely as we have it, but a different selection. Certainly it would seem that different parts of the Old Testament were given different values by different groups within first-century Judaism. The attempt, then, to connect the two Testaments simply by a historical process is weak in that it might not be exactly our Old Testament that was valued by the groups with whom Jesus grew up, or which provided the dominant influence on him.

The 'historical connections' approach can be based more on historical continuity than on textual continuity. In that case, the argument runs something like this: in order to understand Jesus, who is a Jew, we need to understand the historical roots to which he gave allegiance. The Old Testament is the key document for providing us with this understanding. The more difficult issue is whether it can be established, by historical methods, that this special position for the Old Testament is more than a simple accident of history (that is, whether it was essential for God's plan), so that the connection between the two Testaments can be given theological significance. If not, then while the Old Testament may help us to understand Jesus, it has no direct link to our faith.

This position can be further modulated along the lines that the Old Testament provides us with the cultural, religious and especially conceptual and linguistic framework that is necessary for a proper understanding of the message and mission of Jesus, as well as much else in the New Testament. Such phrases as 'kingdom of God' and 'Son of Man', as well as terms like 'Lord' and 'righteousness', can be appreciated properly only with a keen knowledge of the Old Testament. This does seem to be a position that, while valid, does not go far enough by itself to establish that the Old Testament is *theologically* significant for us.

'The God who acts'

A further development of the history-based approach is via the understanding of history (and revelation) that is provided within the Old Testament. This approach was popularized by people such as the American scholar Ernest Wright as 'the God who acts'. The claim was that the Old Testament presents an understanding of both God and history which is unique to the biblical faith and which contrasts with and challenges our Enlightenment-driven definition of history as being devoid of the possibility of God's intervention.

There are a number of difficulties with this approach. The first is the extent to which describing the Old Testament God as 'the God who acts' does justice to the text's overall testimony. Secondly, there is the issue of where this divine action is located. Is it in the real world of human past events, as reconstructed using historical methodologies, or is it only in the 'past events' presented to us by Israel through her confessions of faith? Or is God revealed in the process of recital or reworking of the traditions by the people who helped to produce the Old Testament? These issues raise problems both in reading the Old Testament for itself and when we try to link the two Testaments.

'Salvation history'

While the 'God who acts' approach was promulgated mainly by Americans and some British scholars, the Germans had their own version, which we translate as 'salvation history'. This was grounded in an attempt to understand how Israel handled history. The basic conclusion was that she valued a small number of happenings as special and determinative moments in her experience, such as the exodus, the giving of the law at Sinai, the deliverance of Jerusalem from Sennacherib and the return from exile in Babylon. These events gave meaning to the whole of her history, and they were special because in them God was seen to be at work in a distinctive way. The events were constantly reworked and retold to sustain Israel in difficult times, to help her reach appropriate decisions about how society should be ordered, and to give her clues about how to handle the changing historical and political circumstances. They also provided the focal points for her worship and her profound understanding of the character and nature of God, his relationship to Israel and therefore her own self-understanding.

Scholars perceived that these events were not presented as simply taking place, as though their status as significant events, or their meaning, was obvious. Rather, it was because there was a prophetic voice involved that Israel came to recognize their true value. So, in the case of the exodus, it was important not simply because it happened, but because, as portrayed in the text, Moses announced that it would happen. Even when the event had taken place, however, it still seemed to have its own life, so the exodus became a source of hope for the people in exile in Babylon.

Then, as scholars looked at the New Testament, especially the events of Jesus' life, they saw a similar process at work. They could see that events from the Old Testament now gave meaning not primarily to Israel but to all peoples and to all history, as, for instance, the exodus took on a new significance with the death of Jesus. In turn, the death of Jesus became a powerful 'happening' that still awaits completion (unlike normal events). They could see a historical narrative unfolding, which is about God rescuing, but which is also set within political and historical circumstances and is not an abstraction or a free-floating myth.

Further, the New Testament itself presented the events of the Old Testament as finding resolution in Jesus' life, death and resurrection. One significant difference between the two Testaments is that whereas, for the Old Testament, the focus is the event (although people like Moses clearly contributed to the event), in the New Testament the person of Jesus takes centre stage. The interpreter (the prophetic word) and the interpreted (the event) become synonymous as the revelation of God.

The fivefold drama

A simplified version of the linkage between the Old Testament and the New has been developed by N.T. Wright, in terms of the history or story that the Bible presents through its canonical form, which seems presupposed even when it is not overt. The biblical story can be understood as a drama in (at least) five acts:

- Creation
- Fall
- Israel
- Christ
- Church (including today)

Eschaton (that is, the final end, described in a variety of ways within the Bible, such as the new creation or the return of Christ) is sometimes presented as the final scene of Act 5 and sometimes as a separate epilogue, or Act 6, by those who make use of Wright's construction.

Wright maintains that this concept enables Christians to do justice both to the continuities and discontinuities of the two Testaments. He claims that it also meets some of the challenges of postmodernity, in that it recognizes that the Bible is in effect a text to be performed, like a drama script, and not something to be read like an abstract textbook. Christians today are called to live in and live out the penultimate scene of Act 5. The Bible presents human life and all creation as a story created by God. The plot and the final scene are fixed by God and, in some ways, the characters are provided, but God allows his characters (who are now ourselves) to act freely within the parameters of the big drama.

This concept has several attractive features. It allows for the Old Testament to move towards Christ without making the actual form of Christ's appearance a necessity driven by the Old Testament. It provides for discontinuities, blind alleys and continuities between the Testaments. It can handle the sense of *eschaton* (the drama does come to an end, and it is only from this end that we can make sense of the plot and the details) and still allow a real significance for the historical process in which we are placed.

One of its weaknesses is the extent to which it really does justice to the variety and complexity of biblical material. How do we know that this fivefold drama is presupposed by all the authors and, if it isn't, then by what authority can we or should we force texts through this grid? Despite these criticisms, Wright's account has enabled many Christians to gain a new respect for the Old Testament.

The God who speaks

A rather different focus is to emphasize how, in the Old Testament, God is a God who speaks to Israel (both the nation as a whole and groups and individuals). In recent times, this view has gained a new vitality through the understanding that words do more than communicate information. They 'act'; they perform; they do things. If someone speaks to me in the right way, their words help to give me a sense of value, of what it is to be a person or even to feel love. If someone makes a promise or gives an order, something has happened; it is not simply that words have been spoken. Clearly, the Old Testament provides a picture of a God who speaks to Israel in all kinds of ways, uttering threats that come to pass, issuing laws that institute justice, speaking as the lover-saviour who woos and rescues, and as the partner who calls the other into dialogue, and so on.

In the New Testament, we can see the importance of 'The Word became flesh' (John 1:14, NRSV): it is the story of a God who now speaks with a human voice (although much of the Old Testament presents God as speaking with human words too). Through this enacted 'Word', God accomplishes something new, but it is the same voice that we can recognize in both Testaments.

Linking concepts: calling, grace, sin, forgiveness

In some ways, the suggestion that the two Testaments are linked by their concepts sounds superficial. Time and time again, however, we find that we need to look to the Old Testament, rather than to the Greek-speaking world of the first century AD, if we want to appreciate the riches of the New Testament and understand it correctly. This may seem strange on the surface, in that the language of the New Testament is Greek, but concepts such as calling, righteousness, covenant, grace, forgiveness and redemption make more sense and resonate far more profoundly when considered in the light of their Old Testament equivalents. Many of these concepts can be appreciated in their fullness only in the knowledge of the Old Testament's stories through which they gain their meaning. In order to appreciate how the New Testament works, we need to absorb the Old as well.

Is the converse true—namely that in order to understand the fullness of the Old Testament's concepts, we need to appreciate how they unravel in the New Testament? That is the position of Christians who maintain that the New Testament is the fulfilment of the Old.

CONCLUSION

Here are some of the significant questions that emerge from this short survey of how Old Testament scholars have looked at its connection with the New Testament:

- What are the features that link the Testaments, and how fundamental are they to our faith?
- For such links to be valid, must they apply comprehensively to all parts of the Testaments, or can they be partial?
- Can we understand the Old Testament in its own terms (linguistic, historical and theological) and still see profound connections to the New, or must we impose Christian views on the Old Testament texts for them to be valuable for this purpose?
- Can the Old Testament provide us with helpful and appropriate ways of thinking about God (or even ways of doing theology, handling traditions and relating to history) that are nevertheless incomplete and therefore require closure? If so, does the New Testament provide this closure?
- Can the New Testament provide appropriate ways to understand its connections with the Old Testament? If so, do these understandings become mandatory for us, or are they inapplicable because of our more 'historical' way of reading the Old Testament?
- Is it simply an accident of history that Jesus was a Jew, or is this fact theologically fundamental? Similarly, is it an accident of history that the texts we call the Old Testament were given canonical status, or is it theologically fundamental?

- Does the incorporation of the Old Testament into the Christian canon indicate a special relationship between the Old Testament (and Judaism) and the New Testament (and Christianity), or does it indicate a relationship between all religions (and all history) and the New Testament (and Christianity)?
- Could we really make sense of the New Testament without deep-level familiarity with the Old? If this is not the case, why not? Why is the Old Testament so crucial for the New and therefore for the Christian faith?

While this survey shows that there is a wide range of approaches to the issue of how the two Testaments should be related to one another, it also indicates how difficult it is to make sense of them as belonging together within the one Christian Bible, if there is not a strong link. Probably we should consider that the links are multiple rather than having to choose one or another approach. The connection between the Testaments is like a rope with different coloured strands rather than a single thread. As we read different parts of the Old Testament, we can look for the ways in which each part flows into the New. In doing this, as long as we do not treat the Old Testament as though it were the New, we shall be enriching our understanding of the former as well as deepening our appreciation of the latter.

NOTES

1 A.H.J. Gunneweg, *Understanding the Old Testament* (SCM Press, 1978), p. 227.
2 Although the usual understanding of these terms is that the 'type' is a symbol and the 'antitype' is the reality being foreshadowed by that symbol, they have been reversed here to reflect the original Greek meaning of the words. The *tupos* was a die or stamp, and the *antitupos* was the impression made in wax (for example) by the stamp. Hence the antitype is a lesser reality—a 'shadow' of the type.
3 J.R. Middleton and B.J. Walsh (SPCK, 1995), pp. 130–136.

Chapter 12

THE SERVANT OF CHRIST

From the Christian faith perspective, we can consider the Old Testament as a servant to Christ. We should remember this whenever we read the Old Testament, but also whenever we make use of the insights we have gleaned from this book, both for ourselves and others. It is more than a statement about the Old Testament's relationship to the New, for it is a reminder that we should seek to use the Old Testament, and the many insights and challenges it provides, humbly and constructively rather than as a way of parading our knowledge. While it is true that a growing appreciation of the Old Testament should enhance our sensitivity towards and understanding of both the New Testament and our own faith, we are called to use any gifts we may have to serve the body of Christ and her mission. To treat our insights in any other way would be to act contrary to the Old Testament itself.

The suggestion that the Old Testament should function as a servant to Christ is also, however, a claim about the relationships between the Testaments. In the previous chapter, we surveyed a variety of ways in which scholars have attempted to do justice to both the continuity and the discontinuity implied by the words 'Old Testament'. It should now be clear that these various approaches are not absolutely distinct and that elements from one can be brought to strengthen or expand others. We need to bear in mind all of these approaches, and indeed others, when we are seeking to understand the links between the Old and New Testaments. The Old Testament is a fascinating document, containing in its own right much to intrigue and attract us, as well as being a necessary ingredient for an enriched understanding of the New Testament. By speaking of it as a 'servant', we do not imply that it has no valid existence of its own: any servant can be at work before the arrival of his master, and can have thoughts and feelings that are not controlled by the master, but in the end the servant's true purpose is realized in the context of the master.

Some of the parables told by Jesus refer to the length of the master's absence, but still the significance of the servants and the appropriateness of their behaviour relates to the master. He tells stories such as the one contrasting the behaviour of the faithful and unfaithful servants (Matthew 24:45–51), or about the three servants entrusted with money by their master and what they did with it (Matthew 25:14–30). Indeed, one of the advantages of the Old Testament over the New is the length of time it covers (more than 1000 years). This longer perspective can serve as a resource for us as we continue the Christian journey, 2000 years on.

Throughout this book, the image of visiting a cathedral has been a background metaphor for exploring the Old Testament. As we conclude, it is worth returning to that metaphor. However wonderful the cathedral in terms of the magnificence of the architecture, the richness of the musical tradition, the efficiency of the administration, the friendliness of the welcome, or even the quality of the food in the refectory, the real test is the depth and passion of the worship and mission that the cathedral facilitates, and how well they serve Christ.

I hope that this book will have opened your eyes to some of the riches within the Old Testament, from aspects of its literature and history to its value as a resource for tackling some intractable human dilemmas, and the inspiring insights it offers into the nature of God and human beings. I hope that you will want to return to the Old Testament often and bring your friends along too; I hope that you will want to explore it in much more detail, for a whole lifetime is inadequate to appreciate it all. You will never exhaust its riches or its fascination. In the end, though, unless it leads you to a deeper and fuller understanding of Christ and participation in his mission today, then I suggest that you will have missed the best. The Old Testament does not present itself to us as a testimony to Israel's brilliance but to the God who called her and sustained her and, in the fullness of time, entrusted his Son to her.

QUESTIONS FOR GROUPS

CHAPTER 1: FIRST IMPRESSIONS:
THE OLD TESTAMENT AS LITERATURE

1. As a group, decide beforehand which of the following Old Testament narratives you will read: Joseph (Genesis 37—47), Samson (Judges 13--16) or the book of Esther. Then, when you meet, either explore your chosen story in terms of its merits as a piece of literature (thinking about plot lines, creation and resolution of tension, characterization, challenges and insights for us) or relate the biblical material to artistic interpretations you know about (music, poetry, drama and so on) and consider how they help to interpret each other—or hinder that interpretation.

2. Allocate to three group members samples of Old Testament poetry, such as David's lament for Saul and Jonathan (2 Samuel 1:17–27), Hannah's plea (1 Samuel 2:1–10), or Psalm 8. Ask them to write an appreciation of the passage as poetry, considering the overall message and tone of voice, the style and imagery, its universal appeal, its emotive power, and how and why it works for us. When the group meets, consider each appreciation in relation to the poem. As a concluding exercise, ask the whole group to summarize the strengths and weaknesses of the Old Testament's use of poetry.

3. Consider the lists in Ezra 2 (and Nehemiah 7) and comment on the importance of knowing your family tree in the light of these passages. Invite any group members who have investigated their family tree to share the experience. Consider together situations where it is helpful or necessary to know your origins in the world.

CHAPTER 2: GAINING PERSPECTIVE

1. As a fun exercise, see how many of your group can list the books of the Old Testament in the right order. Alternatively, have a short quiz, asking questions relating to the order of the books. Then, as a group, consider whether the different order in which the books are presented in the English and Hebrew Bibles has any significance, and if so, what? Invite the group to arrange the books in the order they think would be most helpful, noting the factors that direct this decision (for example, historical date of events referred to, date of writing, subject, or liturgical value).

2. Invite the group to consider what they know about the books of the minor prophets—'The Twelve'. (People could be invited to do preparation on specific books before the group meets.) What factors might have influenced the collection and ordering of these books?

3. Encourage the group to select and read one book from the deutero-canonical books in advance. Then, at the meeting, ask each member to say something about the book they have read: what it's about, or anything they found noteworthy. Alternatively, the whole group could read the same book (or selection of chapters). Either the Wisdom of Solomon or Ecclesiasticus is a good place to start. Then, at the meeting, they can discuss their responses to the material.

CHAPTER 3: WAYS OF READING

1. In your group, first decide either to keep a note of what Old Testament passages are read, used liturgically, or included in preaching over, say, a four-week period; or look at a series of Bible reading notes and note all the occasions when the Old Testament is used or mentioned. Then take two examples and reflect on them in the light of the first three chapters of this book. Consider how they were used and how insights from this book might affect the ways in which you would use those passages.

2. Looking through the Psalms, select at least three that you think would be helpful for either a Christmas, Lent or Pentecost service, and explain why you have chosen them. As a group, you may wish to cover all three

festivals between you, or choose one and compare similarities and differences. In your discussion, use some of the ideas from the first three chapters of this book.

3. Consider either the material about Elijah (1 Kings 16:29 to 2 Kings 2:18) or about Jeremiah (chapters 1—11 will provide an adequate sample), and explain whether you think it is appropriate or not to use this material for a series of sermons about the prophet as a person. Think about why it might be helpful to a congregation today, but also consider any limitations of the material for this purpose. How else could this material be used appropriately in a worship context?

CHAPTER 4: THE OLD TESTAMENT AS A SOURCE FOR ANCIENT NEAR EASTERN HISTORY

1. If you have a member of the group who finds history fascinating, arrange for them to look more carefully at one of the periods of Israel's history mentioned on pages 34–44. They can make use of the books mentioned in the Bibliography (see pages 138–140). Encourage them to highlight any changes to the external pressures on the nations during the time, Israel's social structures, and key religious developments. They should aim to refer to Old Testament materials that provide insights about the period they select. Then ask them to explain their 'history' to you. Others with artistic gifts might wish to provide maps or diagrams to capture some of what is communicated.

2. Read 2 Samuel 5—6, 9, and 11—12. If you have a copy of *The Lion Handbook to the Bible*, refer to it for information about this period and some of the main people mentioned in these chapters. Then consider events in our world over the last ten years or so (or the last ten months or so, if you prefer) and note events, issues and characters in our world that in some way parallel these 'accounts. You can either do this individually or in pairs and then compare your choices as a whole group. Ensure that you explain to one another where you see the parallels.

Alternatively, you could present your information as a scrapbook with newspaper articles and then use the Old Testament material as a commentary on the newspaper story. Again, make sure that other people can see the connections you are making by the comments you provide. If you do this, you might wish to display the results in your church.

3. Read what the Old Testament has to say either about the division of Israel into two kingdoms (see 1 Kings 11—14) or the Babylonian capture of Jerusalem (2 Kings 24—25). Consult other books as well if you wish, and then reflect on historical parallels: for instance, the disintegration of the USSR, or the capture of Baghdad in 2003. Discuss together similarities and differences that strike you.

CHAPTER 5: THE RELIGIOUS LIFE: SACRIFICES AND FESTIVALS

1. As a group, share together any knowledge or experiences you have of other faiths' festivals and celebratory events (including those in Judaism). Do you discern any similarities with Israel's festivals? Are there aspects of any of these celebrations from which the Christian faith community can learn?

2. Do you think that it is positive or negative that the birth of Jesus is associated with Christmas and all that goes with it? Reflect on this in the light of what you have learnt about Israel's festivals.

3. How important is it that we celebrate harvest festivals? Discuss this together and then seek to present your case, based on the Old Testament, as though you were wanting to convince your church's worship planning group or minister. You may want to say that it is no longer needed; you may wish to argue that it is essential; you may want to say that it should change to reflect more clearly some aspect of our faith; or you may want to say, 'Definitely not; it's too pagan!'

CHAPTER 6: LIVING LAWS: THE OLD TESTAMENT AS TORAH

1. In the light of this chapter, first highlight ten interesting points from Nehemiah 8. Then discuss why these are significant for the Old Testament and how they are relevant for our Christian faith.

2. Imagine that your church wants to think creatively about the use of Sundays for the Christian community and the whole neighbourhood. The church leaders have asked your group to prepare a presentation about the significance of the sabbath in the Old Testament as background for this project. You are all well aware that we cannot simply equate sabbath and Sunday, but they are looking to you for insight. Can you agree on what you want to communicate?

3. Discuss together as a group whether it would be helpful for Christian discipleship today if we had our own 'Ten Commandments'. If yes, bearing in mind the Old Testament versions, what would yours cover? If no, how might we provide clear guidance for the Christian community about how our faith should be reflected in a different lifestyle?

CHAPTER 7: ISRAEL AND THE IMPORTANCE OF HISTORICAL REMEMBRANCE

1. Consider Psalms 46—48, 72 and 74, as well as Isaiah 1:1—2:5 and 10—12. Then explore the significance of Zion/Jerusalem for the temple and monarchy, and the Israelites' (especially the priests' and monarchs') understandings of the relationship between God and Jerusalem (which included the temple and kingship). What dangers might there be in these understandings? You might find it helpful to use a commentary or a book like *The Lion Handbook to the Bible*, or at least a concordance to provide you with some background and richer biblical material.

2. Construct either a psalm of thanksgiving or of warning, or a passage in the style of the prophets, which reflects on an experience of God's apparent goodness to us as a nation, maybe using as a focus the Second World War, the end of the 'Cold War', the Gulf War or the Iraq War. Use this passage to encourage or challenge one another to live in a more God-honouring way today.

3. In Genesis 12:1–3, God makes several promises to Abraham, including the promise of a homeland. Discuss how this promise may have encouraged people and helped to shape how they understood the way

God wanted them to live at different times in Israel's history. Among the critical times you might want to consider are the moment when they were about to enter Canaan (after the wilderness wanderings), and the period during which they were exiled in Babylon.

CHAPTER 8: DYNAMIC VOICES: THE CONTRIBUTION OF THE PROPHETS

1. Construct a dramatic piece to highlight some important aspects of prophecy, using either Amos' confrontation with Amaziah (Amos 7, especially verses 10–17), Jeremiah's scroll being read to King Jehoiakim (Jeremiah 36, especially verses 20–30) or another passage of your choice. There are many ways to do this, ranging from asking people to improvise different roles while others note down the points that emerge, to studying the passage with the help of commentaries and then carefully scripting the drama together. Alternatively, you could ask one person to write a script, then get the others either to critique it or to read it dramatically and consider their responses to it.

2. Consider together what made prophets a particularly appropriate way for God to challenge and correct his people in their time. Whom might God use in our day for similar purposes, and why?

3. Discuss in your group how we should distinguish true and false prophets, both for the Old Testament and today.

CHAPTER 9: ENGAGING THE CULTURE: EXAMINING WISDOM WITHIN THE BIBLE

1. Why might Psalm 127 be thought of as a 'Wisdom' psalm? Among the issues you may want to include in your discussions are the subjects it deals with, the kind of insights it offers and the way it is structured.

2. Do you think the Old Testament would be better off without the book of Job? Make a list of pros and cons and then take a vote.

3. In the light of what you have learnt about Wisdom material, encourage everyone to write comments on up to ten verses that they select from Proverbs 28. Then share these reflections together. (It is probably a good idea to agree to use the same translation, as there are some rather different accounts of some verses.)

CHAPTER 10: MONOTHEISM, MISSION AND MESSIAH

1. In the light of Deuteronomy 6, especially verses 4–9, and the impact these verses have had throughout the Old Testament, present the case:
   a) that Christians must be allowed to proclaim and share their faith openly; **or**
   b) that Christians only believe in one God; **or**
   c) that in a multi-faith society, several religions, not only Christianity, should be taught in our schools.

In some groups, this could be presented as a three-cornered debate. Do ensure, however, that those who speak make use of the biblical passage mentioned above.

2. Look at the Old Testament passages mentioned under the 'Messiah' section (pp. 107–111), plus others that you may know from Christmas services or elsewhere if you wish. Do you think that a single picture emerges or can be legitimately constructed of either a person or of their mission?

CHAPTER 11: OLD *AND* NEW: A LEGITIMATE CONNECTION?

1. In the light of the different ways of relating the two Testaments, explain to one another which you prefer and why you think your choice is insightful for Christians wanting to appreciate the role that the Old Testament can play in how they live out their beliefs. Indicate any weaknesses or disadvantages you see with your choice as well.

2. Working in twos or threes, select a passage from the Old Testament and then:

a) prepare a sermon outline; **or**
b) prepare a set of notes for a home/study group; **or**
c) describe how this passage could be used to express its significance in other ways: for example, a flower festival, an art competition or storytelling.

Whichever you choose, explain what you are hoping to achieve, how you would evaluate 'success' and why you think this is an appropriate Christian use of the Old Testament.

Share your work within the whole group and consider how you could turn your preparation into something that might help your church or the wider community to appreciate the Old Testament more.

CHAPTER 12: THE SERVANT OF CHRIST

1. Either ask for three volunteers to explain what they have enjoyed and valued from this book or, as a group, talk through the ways in which working through the book has enriched your understanding of the Christian faith. Consider three practical applications that might follow from your appreciation.

2. Think of a way in which you could use what you have learnt and enjoyed from this book and the group discussions to 'serve' the rest of your church. For instance, you could write a short review for your church newsletter, mentioning a couple of insights that you have found valuable.

3. In Luke 24:26–27, Jesus explains that the scriptures indicate that the Messiah must suffer before entering his glory. As you review the journey that the Old Testament presents to us, select an episode, event or passage that illustrates either the suffering or the glory (or both) of God's servants.

BIBLIOGRAPHY

GENERAL

P. & D. Alexander (ed.), *The Lion Handbook to the Bible* (3rd Edition, 1999). For the non-specialist, this is the most useful tool of which I am aware, and deals fully with the Old Testament. The articles are succinct but insightful; the photographs and diagrams stimulate the imagination and often save many words; the brief introduction and notes to each book ensure that the user always has something with which to gain a start.

David Spriggs, *Feasting on God's Word* (BRF, 2002). This provides a variety of ways of engaging with the Bible, many of which involve our imaginative and artistic skills.

OLD TESTAMENT

E. Charpentier, *How to Read the Old Testament* (SCM, 1982). Although relatively old now, this is a useful complement to the approach that I have taken in this book.

John Drane, *Introduction to the Old Testament* (Lion, 2000).

For those who wish to explore different sections of the Old Testament, the series *Exploring the Old Testament* (SPCK) is a good place to start. The volumes available at the moment are:
  Vol. 1: *The Pentateuch*, G.J. Wenham (2003)
  Vol. 3: *The Psalms and Wisdom Literature*, E. Lucas (2003)
  Vol. 4: *The Prophets*, G.M. McConville (2002)

COMMENTARIES

For those who wish to explore particular books of the Old Testament, a useful series is *The People's Bible Commentary* (BRF). Designed to 'warm the heart as well as stimulate the mind', this series is based on good scholarship. The following volumes are available at the moment:

- Mike Butterworth, *Leviticus and Numbers* (2003)
- Steven Mathewson, *Joshua and Judges* (2003)
- Robert Fyall, *Ruth, Esther, Ecclesiastes, Song of Songs and Lamentations* (2005)
- Harry Mowvley, *1 & 2 Samuel* (1998)
- Stephen Dawes, *1 & 2 Kings* (2001)
- Michael Tunnicliffe, *Chronicles to Nehemiah* (1999)
- Katharine Dell, *Job* (2002)
- Donald Coggan, *Psalms 1—72* (1998)
- Donald Coggan, *Psalms 73—150* (1999)
- Enid Mellor, *Proverbs* (1999)
- Rex Mason, *Jeremiah* (2002)
- Ernest Lucas, *Ezekiel* (2002)
- Paula Gooder, *Hosea to Micah* (2005)
- Grace Emerson, *Nahum to Malachi* (1998)

Another useful introductory series for individual books is the *Tyndale Old Testament Commentaries*, General Editor D.J. Wiseman, published by IVP.

MORE SPECIALIST BOOKS

For those who have become fascinated by the Old Testament and want to discover whether they would find more specialist study equally enthralling, here are a few suggestions, deliberately chosen to provide very different approaches.

John Barton, *Old Testament—Method in Biblical Study* (DLT 1984). This explores, in a readable way, how different approaches to the Old Testament arose and what they can contribute, and evaluates their strengths and weaknesses.

William P. Brown, *Seeing the Psalms* (Westminster John Knox, 2002). This seeks to unpack the theology of the Psalms via literary investigation (linked to archaeology), particularly some key metaphors.

Walter Brueggemann, *Theology of the Old Testament* (Fortress Press, 1997). Brueggemann is a passionate scholar who is unafraid of controversy. It is generally agreed that this work broke the mould as far as Old Testament theologies are concerned.

Roy S. Clements, *Wisdom in Theology* (Paternoster, 1992). This explores the Wisdom materials and themes from the perspective of people in exile, awaiting a new future, using the concept of liminality: being at the doorway.

★ ALSO BY DAVID SPRIGGS ★

FEASTING ON GOD'S WORD

From frozen food to gourmet banquet

The Bible is a neglected treasure—one that we ignore at our peril—yet fewer and fewer people read it these days, not only in wider society but even in the Christian community. This book is written to reverse that trend, to motivate Christians of all ages to experience the power of the Bible in new ways.

Packed with imaginative suggestions for enjoying the Bible, from 'Eat it' to 'Display it' to 'Twist it', this is a book that will help us turn the 'frozen food' of scripture into a gourmet banquet, at which we can sit down to feast on God.

ISBN 1 84101 222 X   £6.99
Available from your local Christian bookshop or, in case of difficulty, direct from BRF using the order form on page 143.

THE STORY WE LIVE BY

A reader's guide to the New Testament

R. ALASTAIR CAMPBELL

At the heart of Christianity is a story—not a code nor a creed, but the story of Jesus. Christians have lived by this story for centuries and return to it again and again to renew faith and deepen understanding. This book is an accessible introduction to how that story is presented in the New Testament, firstly in the four different accounts of Jesus' life, death and resurrection, followed by the early years of the Church and the ensuing series of letters and commentaries on those events.

Starting with an analysis of the four Gospels, *The Story We Live By* shows how the New Testament writers shaped their material to communicate the truth of Jesus' teaching to their audiences, and how their writings arise from and still maintain continuity with the Old Testament. It also covers issues such as authorship, textual dating and the different literary forms used from sermons to apocalypse.

ISBN 1 84101 359 5   £12.99
Available from your local Christian bookshop or, in case of difficulty, direct from BRF using the order form on page 143.

ORDER FORM

REF	TITLE	PRICE	QTY	TOTAL
222 X	*Feasting on God's Word*	£6.99		
359 5	*The Story We Live By*	£12.99		

POSTAGE AND PACKING CHARGES					
order value	UK	Europe	Surface	Air Mail	Postage and packing:
£7.00 & under	£1.25	£3.00	£3.50	£5.50	Donation:
£7.01–£30.00	£2.25	£5.50	£6.50	£10.00	**Total enclosed:**
Over £30.00	free	prices on request			

Name _____ Account Number _____

Address _____

_____ Postcode _____

Telephone Number _____ Email _____

Payment by: Cheque ❏ Mastercard ❏ Visa ❏ Postal Order ❏ Switch ❏

Credit card no. ❏❏❏❏ ❏❏❏❏ ❏❏❏❏ ❏❏❏❏   Expires ❏❏ ❏❏

Switch card no. ❏❏❏❏❏❏❏❏❏❏❏❏❏❏❏❏❏❏

Issue no. of Switch card ❏❏❏❏   Expires ❏❏ ❏❏

Signature _____ Date _____

All orders must be accompanied by the appropriate payment.

Please send your completed order form to:
BRF, First Floor, Elsfield Hall, 15–17 Elsfield Way, Oxford OX2 8FG
Tel. 01865 319700 / Fax. 01865 319701 Email: enquiries@brf.org.uk

❏ Please send me further information about BRF publications.

Available from your local Christian bookshop.   BRF is a Registered Charity

brf

Resourcing your spiritual journey

through...

- Bible reading notes
- Books for Advent & Lent
- Books for Bible study and prayer
- Books to resource those working with under 11s in school, church and at home

- Quiet days and retreats
- Training for primary teachers and children's leaders
- Godly Play
- Barnabas Live

For more information, visit the **brf** website at **www.brf.org.uk**